British Prime Ministers

A Very Peculiar History®

'I have climbed to the top of the greasy pole.'

Benjamin Disraeli
on first becoming Prime Minister

For Rosie, Jack and Beth, long-term
observers of 'the political situation'.

DA

Editor: Nick Pierce
Artist: David Lyttleton
Additional artwork: Shutterstock

Published in Great Britain in MMXX by
Book House, an imprint of
The Salariya Book Company Ltd
25 Marlborough Place, Brighton BN1 1UB
www.salariya.com

ISBN: 978-1-912904-68-6

Visit
www.salariya.com
for our online catalogue and
free fun stuff.

British Prime Ministers
A Very Peculiar History®

Written by
David Arscott

Created and designed by
David Salariya

BOOK HOUSE
a SALARIYA imprint

'Tell me of any Prime Minister who has become sick of his power. They become sick of the *want* of power when it's falling away from them'
Lady Palliser in Anthony Trollope's
The Prime Minister

'The House of Commons is a great unwieldy body which requires great art and some cordial to keep it loyal'
Henry Pelham

'An extraordinary affair. I gave them their orders and they wanted to stay and discuss them.'
Duke of Wellington after his first Cabinet meeting as Prime Minister

'In this country we prefer rule by amateurs'
Clement Attlee

'The politician who never makes a mistake never made a decision'
John Major

Contents

In war you can only be killed once, but in politics many times.

FIRST AMONG EQUALS

Our story begins with a country fearful of tyrannical rulers, with a German king who could muster scarcely a word of the English language and with a ruthless political operator who shamelessly manipulated the House of Commons through the corrupt use of patronage.

From these fraught beginnings a fledgling British democracy would develop into a constitution mirrored in countries around the world, with power in parliament wielded by the dominant political party under the leadership of that first among equals, the prime minister.

Power struggles

The Stuart king Charles I lost his head in 1649, having been deemed treasonably dictatorial, and although his son Charles II was welcomed back to the throne in 1660, parliament was determined to retain the whip hand ever after.

Charles was succeeded by his brother, the Catholic James II, but he was deposed within four years, largely because of his religious intolerance.* In 1688 the birth of his son (another James) sparked fears of a Catholic dynasty, and in what became known as the Glorious Revolution, his daughter Mary, a Protestant, was invited to share the throne with her Dutch husband, William of Orange.

Mary's sister Anne succeeded to the throne in 1702 and on her death twelve years later – by which time England and Scotland had been united as the kingdom of Great Britain – Parliament found a suitable Protestant successor in her German cousin, George of Hanover. He ruled as George I.

---

* Attempts to restore James and his descendants to the throne (the so-called Jacobite rebellions) would persist for more than half a century.

8

The shrewd political fixer was Robert Walpole (1676–1745), the man all commentators now agree was the country's first *de facto* prime minister, even though the term was regarded as an insult at the time – suggesting that he was rather getting above himself – and it wasn't until 1878, in a treaty signed by Disraeli, that an incumbent officially gave himself the title.

Walpole's actual rank (which prime ministers retain to this day) was First Lord of the Treasury. For more than twenty years he was the vital oiler of wheels between the king and parliament in order to raise cash and win support for the monarch's programmes.

'Every man has his price'

He wasn't exactly the smoothest of operators. Although educated at Eton and Cambridge, he liked to play the role of the bluff, hunting country squire and was known for his coarse manners and poor personal hygiene.

But he was the sharpest. The cynical quote above is often attributed to him – and whether he said it or not, that was his guiding belief.

His world, to be fair to him, was very different from ours. There were no paid MPs (not until 1911 in fact), and many were propelled into the Commons by landowners and peers who controlled 'rotten boroughs' up and down the land and used them to their advantage.

A position in government was the way to turn a seat at Westminster into a serious money-earner, and who else but the canny Walpole could elevate needy MPs into such lucrative positions? Handsome backhanders were the order of the day.

If enriching himself * had been his only concern he wouldn't have lasted long. What Walpole achieved for the king was a long period of political stability with three basic aims:

- Keeping taxes low
- Promoting trade
- Avoiding war

* As he certainly did. He built a Palladian mansion at Houghton Hall in Norfolk (now open to the public), stocking it with hundreds of Old Master paintings. These were later sold to Catherine the Great and can be seen at the Hermitage Museum in St Petersburg.

The Beggar's Opera

The early eighteenth century was a time of bawdy raucousness in public life, with artists and writers irreverently lampooning the vices of the powerful.

An engraving of 1740 ('Idol Worship, or The Way to Preferment') shows Walpole's outsized naked rump blocking the gate to the treasury, with his ministers obliged to kiss it before being allowed to enter.

In 1728 John Gay, encouraged by his friends Jonathan Swift and Alexander Pope, wrote *The Beggar's Opera*, a satire on both high falutin' Italian opera and on the corruption of what Walpole's detractors called his 'Robinocracy' – Robin being one of the short forms of his first name.

The three-acter was so bitingly successful that in 1737 Walpole had a Licensing Act passed in parliament, ruling that every new play had to be passed by the lord chamberlain before it could be performed.

That Act survived until 1968, when it was repealed by Roy Jenkins, the home secretary in Harold Wilson's Labour government.

Whigs and Tories

There were as yet no party 'machines', with whips to force rebels into line (money, as we've seen, did most of the talking), but MPs fell into two broad groups from the Georgian period until the mid nineteenth century.

The **Whigs** opposed absolute monarchy. While not democratic in the modern sense, they believed in broader suffrage rights, Catholic emancipation and the abolition of slavery.

The early **Tories** were supporters of the Crown, opposing the removal of James II. After a long period of Whig domination, the party was revived under Pitt the Younger, when it became the embodiment of tradition, 'God, King and Country'.

Both parties later split. Reformist Whigs and Tories combined to form the **Liberal Party** – a major player until the rise of the **Labour Party** in the early twentieth century. The rump of the Tories became the **Conservative Party** (today, somewhat confusingly, still commonly known as the Tories).

What Walpole did for parliament was to flex its considerable muscles in dealings with the Crown. The monarch could replace his first lord of the treasury on a whim (he would retain that power until the Great Reform Bill of 1832), but that was never going to happen under George I.

The King spent as much time as he reasonably could back home in Hanover – he died there – and he not only had little patience with handling day-to-day affairs (he rarely attended meetings of the cabinet), but was severely handicapped by his poor grasp of English.

As Walpole likewise had no German, the pair were obliged to conduct their business in what must have been a highly comical dog Latin.

On the king's death in 1727 Walpole was set to be fired, because George II didn't like him, but reality soon dawned: not only did the great wheeler-dealer have a solid majority in the House, but (money again) he had engineered a generous increase in the civil list – the annual sum parliament granted the monarch for his official expenditure. Back to business as usual!

Walpole nurtured a useful friendship with Queen Caroline,* and George came to value Walpole so much that he offered him a large house in Downing Street as his London base – a gift he accepted on condition that it was to belong not to him personally but to whoever held the post of first lord of the treasury.

He later gave some frank advice on managing the king to the next prime minister but one, Henry Pelham:

> Plain truths will not be relished at first in opposition to prejudices, conceived and infused in favour of his own partialities; and you must dress up your offer with the appearance of no other view or tendency but to promote his service in his own way, to the utmost of your power. And the more you can make anything appear to be his own, and agreeable to his declaration and orders, given to you before he went, the better you will be heard.

---

* The friendship was tested when someone told her that the foul-mouthed Walpole had called her a fat bitch, but after he secured an increase in the civil list she sent a message that 'the fat bitch has forgiven him'.

Walpole was, by his own admission, 'no saint, no spartan, no reformer', and it was inevitable that his enemies would close in on him once he showed signs of weakness.

His first bruising came in 1733, when his Excise Bill to eliminate smuggling proved so unpopular that he had to abandon it altogether.

A different breed

Although Walpole had six children by his wife, Catherine, he spent most of his time with his much younger mistress, the beautiful and witty Maria Skerrett. He married her on Catherine's death, but within months Maria, too, had died.

Walpole's youngest son, Horace, was given three sinecures by his father to ensure that he never had to worry about money. He represented a rotten borough in parliament, but his leaning was to the arts rather than to politics. He's known today for writing the early Gothic novel *The Castle of Otranto* and for creating Strawberry Hill, his Gothic revival villa in Twickenham, south-west of London.

PM fact file 1

Served longest term: Walpole (1721–1742) 20 years, 315 days
Shortest term: Rockingham (1782) 97 days*
Fewest days in office overall: Canning (1827) 119 days
Most terms: Gladstone, 4
Served under most sovereigns: Baldwin, 3
Sovereigns with most PMs:
  George III, 14
  Elizabeth II, 14
  Victoria, 10
Most general elections contested: Asquith, 6
Youngest on election: Pitt the Younger, 24
Youngest on leaving office: Grafton, 34
Oldest on first election: Palmerston, 70
Oldest on any election: Gladstone, 82
Longest lived: Callaghan, 92
Shortest lived: Devonshire, 44
Survived longest time after office:
  Grafton, 41 years
Survived shortest time after office:
  Campbell-Bannerman, 18 days

* Lord Bath in 1746 (2 days) and Earl Waldegrave in 1756 (4 days) were both appointed by George II but were unable to form governments, while Wellington's 'caretaker administration' in 1834 (25 days) was an acknowledged stopgap arrangement.

More damaging still was the outbreak of the delightfully named War of Jenkins' Ear against Spain in 1739. Not only had Walpole strived to prevent it ('They are ringing their bells – soon they will be wringing their hands' he is reported to have said when a gung-ho public rejoiced), but the war began badly and his reputation never recovered.

He managed to cling on to power until 1742, when he lost control of the Commons. He resigned and was elevated to the House of Lords.

Legacy

Close on three hundred years have passed since Walpole began his domination of public affairs in Britain, but it's not fanciful to regard him as the flag bearer for the much developed system we know today.

After all, the parliamentary power which the Whigs were determined to enforce against the Crown – a policy which he so ruthlessly pursued – has only intensified with the passage of time.

Here are a few of the powers invested in the sovereign today:

- **To appoint and dismiss the prime minister**
- **To summon and dissolve parliament**
- **To declare war and command the army**
- **To issue royal pardons**

The ghosts of the Hanover Georges might rejoice if they came across that list, but it would have to be explained to them that it was all a glorious sham.

Royal perks

Despite the great shift in the balance of power over the centuries, British sovereigns have rights denied to mere prime ministers.

Most important of all, they're above the law, and therefore free from prosecution or civil action in the courts.

They're exempt from needing a driving licence or a passport, and they never paid tax until in 1992, at a time when the royal family's reputation was at a low ebb, the Queen voluntarily started doing so.

On paper (and the fiction is often dressed up in pleasingly ornate flummery), the sovereign has absolute authority over affairs of state. In reality the 'royal prerogative' is a kind of licence granted by parliament – and if any king or queen showed signs of thwarting the will of the Commons, the monarchy itself would be in serious danger of abolition.

People power

This might suggest that prime ministers have become all-powerful figures. In reality they face a challenge that Walpole never had to worry about – winning the all-too-fickle support of the man and woman in the street.

Keeping control of your own party can be difficult enough (under the Robinocracy stuffing pockets with cash did the trick, whereas a modern leader's bribes are reduced to threats of demotion and the handing out of knighthoods), but it takes a nimble-footed prime minister to keep a step ahead of trouble when public dissatisfaction is expressed, day after relentless day, in opinion polls, online postings and the popular press.

'In war you can only be killed once, but in politics many times.'

Winston Churchill

The most successful modern prime ministers have contrived to finesse the principles which first drove them into politics with the mood of the electorate and opposition in the House.

But even here there's a danger: get too good at it and you'll be accused of unseemly 'spin'!

One of a team

'Premier' is the common shorthand form for the post, but the less snappy 'first among equals' suits it better.

When the average UK salary is under £30,000 you might regard an income of about £150,000 a year something not to be sneezed at (even if it's far below what many of today's captains of industry demand) – but although it's pitched at roughly twice what an ordinary MP gets, it's only marginally higher than the pay of a top ranking cabinet minister.

So why do they put themselves through it? A cynic will disagree, but most are motivated by a sense of public duty, however mired they later become in the dirty business of political trade-offs in an attempt to retain the trappings of power.

And what brings about their almost inevitable fall from grace? Harold Macmillan is said to have answered that succinctly: 'Events, dear boy, events.'

In these pages we'll enjoy the spectacle of prime ministers through the ages valiantly pitting themselves against the often momentous events of their time. Some emerge in triumph, others in disgrace, but they all play out their entertaining dramas in the unforgiving glare of the public spotlight.

List of Prime Ministers

Several ennobled prime ministers are best known by their titles (few readers would recognise Henry Temple as Lord Palmerston), but we here also give their birth names at the first reference.

Robert Walpole (1721–42) *Whig*
Spencer Compton, Earl of Wilmington (1742–43) *Whig*
Henry Pelham (1743–54) *Whig*
Thomas Pelham–Holles, Duke of Newcastle (1754–56) *Whig*
William Cavendish, Duke of Devonshire (1756–57) *Whig*
Duke of Newcastle (1757–62) *Whig*
John Stuart, Earl of Bute (1762–63) *Tory*
George Grenville (1763–65) *Whig*
Charles Watson-Wentworth, Marquess of Rockingham (1765–66) *Whig*
William Pitt, the Elder (1766–68) *Whig*
August Henry Fitzroy, Duke of Grafton (1768–70) *Whig*
Frederick, Lord North (1770–82) *Tory*
Marquess of Rockingham (1782) *Whig*

William Petty, Earl of Shelburne
(1782–83) *Whig*
William Henry Cavendish-Bentinck,
Duke of Portland (1783) *Whig*
William Pitt, the Younger (1783–1801) *Tory*
Henry Addington, Lord Sidmouth (1801–04)
Tory
William Pitt, the Younger (1804–1806) *Tory*
William, Lord Grenville (1806–07) *Whig*
Duke of Portland (1807–1809) *Tory*
Spencer Perceval (1809–12) *Tory*
Robert Jenkinson, Earl of Liverpool
(1812–27) *Tory*
George Canning (1827) *Tory*
Frederick Robinson, Viscount Goderich
(1827–28) *Tory*
Arthur Wellesley, Duke of Wellington
(1828–30) *Tory*
Charles, Earl Grey (1830–34) *Whig*
William Lamb, Lord Melbourne (1834) *Whig*
Duke of Wellington (1834) *Tory*
Sir Robert Peel (1834–35) *Conservative*
Lord Melbourne (1835–41) *Whig*
Sir Robert Peel (1841–46) *Conservative*
John, Earl Russell (1846–52) *Whig*
Edward Smith-Stanley, Earl of Derby
(1852) *Conservative*

George Hamilton-Gordon, Earl of Aberdeen
(1852–55) *Tory*
Henry Temple, Lord Palmerston
(1855–58) *Whig*
Earl of Derby (1858–59) *Conservative*
Lord Palmerston (1859–65) *Liberal*
Earl Russell (1865–66) *Liberal*
Earl of Derby (1866–68) *Conservative*
Benjamin Disraeli (1868) *Conservative*
William Ewart Gladstone (1868–74) *Liberal*
Benjamin Disraeli (1874–80) *Conservative*
William Ewart Gladstone (1880–85) *Liberal*
Robert Cecil, Lord Salisbury (1885–86)
Conservative
William Ewart Gladstone (1886) *Liberal*
Lord Salisbury (1886–92) *Conservative*
William Ewart Gladstone (1892–94) *Liberal*
Archibald Primrose, Earl of Rosebery
(1894–95) *Liberal*
Lord Salisbury (1895–1902) *Conservative*
Arthur Balfour (1902–05) *Conservative*
Sir Henry Campbell-Bannerman
(1905–08) *Liberal*
Herbert Henry Asquith (1908–16) *Liberal*
David Lloyd George (1916–22) *Liberal*
Andrew Bonar Law (1922–23) *Conservative*
Stanley Baldwin (1923–24) *Conservative*

Ramsay MacDonald (1924) *Labour*
Stanley Baldwin (1924–29) *Conservative*
Ramsay MacDonald (1929–35) *Labour/
National Labour*
Stanley Baldwin (1935–37) *Conservative*
Neville Chamberlain (1937–40) *Conservative*
Sir Winston Churchill (1940–45) *Conservative*
Clement Attlee (1945–51) *Labour*
Sir Winston Churchill (1951–55) *Conservative*
Sir Anthony Eden (1955–57) *Conservative*
Harold Macmillan (1957–63) *Conservative*
Sir Alec Douglas-Home (1963–64)
Conservative
Harold Wilson (1964–70) *Labour*
Edward Heath (1970–74) *Conservative*
Harold Wilson (1974–76) *Labour*
James Callaghan (1976–79) *Labour*
Margaret Thatcher (1979–90) Conservative
John Major (1990–97) *Conservative*
Tony Blair (1997–2007) *Labour*
Gordon Brown (2007–10) *Labour*
David Cameron (2010–16) *Conservative*
Theresa May (2016–2019) *Conservative*
Boris Johnson (2019–) *Conservative*

‘No house in London
has had more spent on
it per square metre,
yet it doesn't *look* as
though money has
been lavished on it.’

CHAPTER ONE

10 DOWNING STREET

George Downing was a political turncoat who, having served as a diplomat for Oliver Cromwell, not only became Charles II's treasury secretary but ran spy rings to hunt down former comrades who had signed Charles I's death warrant.

It is this unpleasant character, described by Pepys in his diary as 'a perfidious rogue', that today's prime ministers have to thank for their London HQ. In the role of property speculator, he hired Sir Christopher Wren to design him a cul-de-sac of terraced houses in the centre of Westminster – and named it Downing Street.

Downing had leased his land from the Crown. When George II handed the keys of what is now no. 10 to Robert Walpole some fifty years later, he also threw in the large mansion behind it (prosaically known as 'The House at the Back') overlooking Horse Guards Parade.

Not content with that, Walpole bought the next door house in the terrace from a Mr Chicken and had the famous architect and landscape designer William Kent connect all three buildings together on two storeys.

Walpole worked on the ground floor, taking the largest room in the north-west corner (now the cabinet office, where his portrait looks down from the wall) for his study.

Gimcrack

As our first premier no doubt quickly found out, Downing's terrace had been jerry-built. Never mind that it had been designed by the architect of St Paul's Cathedral – the houses had been thrown up on boggy ground with only the flimsiest of foundations. This would cause problems for centuries to come.

Floors buckled and cracks developed in the walls and chimneys. As early as 1766 the chancellor of the exchequer, Charles Townshend, ordered extensive repairs after finding 'the Floors & Chimneys much sunk from the level'.

Fourteen years later the Board of Works went further, urging that 'no time be lost in taking down said building', and the *Morning Herald* agreed:

> So much has this extraordinary edifice cost the country, for one moiety [half] of the sum a much better dwelling might have been purchased!

Although the government took over other parts of the terrace, by the late eighteenth century this area so close to parliament had become an insalubrious backwater of dark alleys, frequented by criminals and prostitutes. One by one the houses were allowed to fall into disrepair and were pulled down, and when a fire destroyed the upper floors of no. 12 in 1879 – the stump was saved – only 10 and 11 (traditionally the chancellor of the exchequer's home) were left intact.

Piecemeal rescue operations went on over the generations until at last, during Harold Macmillan's premiership in the early 1960s, the problem was tackled at its root.

By this time the patched-up building was so fragile, and dry rot so invasive, that the number of people allowed on to the upper floors was restricted for fears that the bearing walls would collapse.

Miners digging down into the foundations discovered that the huge supporting timbers had also decayed.

Demolition was once more on the agenda but was again overruled. Nos 10 and 11 were to be substantially renovated and no. 12 rebuilt, and in a three-year transformation costing more than a million pounds, new foundations of steel-reinforced concrete were created up to 5.5m (18ft) below the surface.

The interiors were completely gutted. Although many rooms were reconstructed to keep their appearance of two hundred years before, some 60 per cent of the materials were brand new.

That strange number 10

A curiosity of the famous Downing Street front door* is its skewed zero – now so iconic a feature that it can never be changed.

Bad workmanship is to blame. The architect for the 1960s renovations, Raymond Erith, was 'heartbroken' by cost-cutting changes to his plans and declared the project was 'a frightful waste of money because it just has not been done properly'.

In a letter to the typographical expert James Mosley, he explained that the Ministry of Works had used a version of the carving on the Trajan column in Rome for the door, with the letter O being used for the zero. The job had been completed in a rush, and inexpertly, with no time for him to see it before it was finished.

'I might say,' he wrote bitterly, 'that the mess that was made of the lettering was absolutely nothing in comparison with what happened elsewhere.'

---

* The modern door is made of blast-proof steel rather than wood, and there's one in reserve so that they can be switched every two years for repainting.

And that distinctive facade of black bricks? The work revealed that they were, in fact, yellow and had simply been coated with the grime of the ages. Once cleaned up they were (of course) promptly painted black to satisfy the British fondness for tradition.

Fast forward four decades to the Tony Blair era and – surprise, surprise! – the building was found to be in need of yet more serious work. Dry rot had come back, and had been treated, soon after the 1960s reconstruction, but now it was time for no. 10 to undergo another major upgrade.

- It was no longer weatherproof, with failed lead guttering and cracked brickwork
- The heating system had broken down
- Power outages had become commonplace
- The facade of no. 11 was unstable, and had to be secured by 225 stainless steel pins

'No house in London has had more spent on it per square metre,' the political historian and biographer Anthony Seldon has written, 'yet it doesn't *look* as though money has been lavished on it.'

Somewhat Sniffy

Not that many of our early prime ministers after Walpole were overly keen on it. After all, most of them were exceedingly rich, and apart from their piles in the country they had town houses more than a match for Downing Street, thank you very much.

Until the twentieth century about half the building's potential residents declined to make use of it other than as an office, offering its living space to grateful friends and relatives.

One of the exceptions was Lord North, who lived at no. 10 for a full fifteen years as chancellor of the exchequer and first lord of the treasury. Here he entertained the likes of the controversial soldier, adventurer and multi-millionaire Clive of India*, Dr Johnson of dictionary fame and Thomas Hansard, founder of the parliamentary reporting system still used today.

* *Clive was so frequent a visitor that special furniture was made for him. You can see it in the first floor anteroom and the Terracotta Room.*

Lord North* introduced embellishments which have survived to this day, including the black and white chequerboard floor in the entrance hall, the king's head door knocker and the ornamental lamp above it.

Pitt the Younger, who described no. 10 as 'my vast, awkward house', nevertheless lived there for longer than anyone else (more than twenty years all told), but it was left to later premiers to add their own personal touches.

- **Viscount Goderich had only a brief tenure during the 1820s, but he employed the architect Sir John Soane to fashion the wood-panelled State Dining Room.**

- **Disraeli, finding the place 'dingy and decaying' (nobody had used the living quarters for thirty years), had the State pay for enhancing the public rooms, but forked out himself to improve home comforts such as a hot water supply to his bath.**

He had such a close resemblance to George III that rumour-mongers claimed he was the illegitimate son of the king's deceased father, Prince Frederick – North's godfather.

- In 1894, during Gladstone's occupancy, electricity was supplied to the building and the first telephones were installed. (Central heating would eventually arrive in 1937.)

- Ramsay MacDonald, intent on restoring some former grandeur to the place, created the Prime Minister's Library (originally in the cabinet room, but now on the first floor, overlooking the street), to which premiers and members of their cabinets have donated books ever since.

- In an overhaul of the public rooms in the 1980s, Margaret Thatcher had the architect Quinlan Terry introduce an ornate plasterwork ceiling and Doric columns to the State Drawing Room, a style he thought 'mildly triumphalist and confident' but which English Heritage, who hadn't been consulted, reportedly dismissed as 'naff'.

As so often, however, the so-called Iron Lady had the last word. Carved into the plasterwork above the door into the Panelled Drawing Room is a punning tribute to her for having commissioned the work – a reed-carrying thatcher.

Hidden depths

The TV cameras regularly show us a stream of politicians passing in and out of that no. 10 door, the prime minister sometimes striding out to a lectern in order to announce some vital (or otherwise) government policy, but they offer no clue as to the vastness of the interior.

The entrance hall leads to a warren of about a hundred rooms, via various staircases and corridors – one of these running to the left through the chancellor of the exchequer's home to no. 12 beyond.

The first floor of Downing Street.

The building needs to be large, because it serves three main functions:

- **It's the prime minister's home (on the second floor) – although Tony Blair and David Cameron swapped houses with their chancellors of the exchequer as no. 11 was roomier for their young families.**

On guard

If you're ever invited into no. 10, take a peek at a strange chair with a hood that sits in a corner of the entrance hall. It was designed by Thomas Chippendale (better known for more refined furniture) to provide comfort and shelter for the police officer on guard outside the building, and it even has a drawer underneath for hot coals to keep him warm.

Note, too, the scratches on the right arm – caused by pistols rubbing against the leather.

Until 1989 it was possible for anyone to stroll along Downing Street. In that year, however, the growing threat of terrorist attacks led to the introduction of the sturdy iron security gates which bar the way today.

- It's a working area (chiefly on the ground floor), with a scattering of offices and the Cabinet room – which overlooks the terrace.

- It's a place of entertainment (on the first floor), with three drawing rooms of various sizes and two dining rooms for official functions, the smaller seating a dozen people, the State Dining Room able to seat up to 65 around its U-shaped table.

Chief mouser

Only in Britain, perhaps, would a humble puss carry the title Chief Mouser to the Cabinet Office. A resident four-legged rat-catcher has often been given the run of no. 10 (and with good reason), but a young black-and-white stray – named Humphrey after the cynical, smooth-talking civil servant in the BBC TV series *Yes Minister* –was the first officially to be awarded the honour in 1989.

Humphrey once went missing from Downing Street. On his return he issued a statement through the civil service: 'It is nice to be back, and I am looking forward to the new parliamentary session.'

It's been estimated that a non-political staff some 200-strong (cleaners, cooks, waitresses, gardeners) is employed to keep this impressive show on the road, although when a Freedom of Information request sought the numbers in 2017 the prime minister's office strangely refused to comply.

The prime minister's flat has its own kitchen, sometimes opened up to the television cameras so that its occupant can show the common touch, but a literally 'below stairs' activity visitors rarely see is the preparation of food for State banquets.

Down in the basement, but rising two storeys high and with a huge arched window, is the great kitchen created during restorations in 1783. The work table at its centre is 4.3m (14ft) long, 0.91m (3ft) wide and 130mm (5 inches) thick.

Unhappily it failed to impress the celebrity chef Jamie Oliver when he was invited to cook for a gathering of G2 leaders in 2009. Calling it 'the worst kitchen in England', he threw in an added insult: 'Wandsworth Prison has better gear than Downing Street.'

Chequers

Prime ministers in the twentieth century were no longer drawn from a landowning class endowed with spreading country estates, and their need for a rural retreat was met by Lord Lee of Fareham – soldier, diplomat, MP and patron of the arts – who gave Chequers to the nation late in the First World War.

It's a sixteenth century manor house 65km (40 miles) west of London in Buckinghamshire with a colourful history: Lady Mary Grey, sister of Lady Jane, was confined here for two years after Elizabeth I banished her from court for marrying without permission (her bedroom survives intact), while a large collection of memorabilia testifies to its later connection with Oliver Cromwell's family.

Premiers use it both to relax and to entertain distinguished visitors in an informal setting, and Margaret Thatcher, who visited as often as she could, wrote that nobody could stay at Chequers without falling in love with it.

Don't even think about setting foot in its extensive grounds, though: under the Serious Organised Crime and Police Act it's a criminal offence to trespass on the estate.

Unaware of the clattering pans and gouts of steam in this echoing netherworld, the distinguished guests climb the elegant main staircase with its wrought iron balustrade on their way to one of the ornate dining rooms.

On the yellow ochre walls they see engravings and photographs of every premier from Walpole to the present day – the most recent at the top, but the current incumbent having to await retirement before being added to the gallery.

Margaret Thatcher, when her turn came, noted that her immediate predecessor, James Callaghan, had chosen to have his image displayed in colour, but she wisely plumped for plain black and white.

She was well aware that colour, like reputation, is inclined to fade...

He is a better speaker
than I am, but
thank God! I have
more judgement.

TWO PITTS AND OLD BONEY

They were known as 'the Patriot Boys' – a group of politicians who scorned Walpole's desire for peace among nations and pressed for a show of British naval power.

None of them was as brilliantly outspoken as the pugnacious William Pitt, who very soon got his way with a conflict so widespread that some have called it a forerunner of the First World War. As the nation expanded its territories around the globe, it would fall to the next generation, and to Pitt's equally influential son, to contest the rising menace of revolutionary France and the military genius of Napoleon.

PM fact file 2

Brothers: Henry Pelham and the Duke of Newcastle are the only PM brothers
Father & son: George and William Grenville; and the Pitts, Elder and Younger
Born outside the British Isles: Bonar Law
Most general elections contested: 6, Asquith
Never fought a general election: 14
Earl of Wilmington, Duke of Devonshire, Earl of Bute, George Grenville, Duke of Grafton, Lord Rockingham, Lord Shelburne, Spencer Perceval, George Canning, Viscount Goderich, Lord Aberdeen, Earl of Rosebery, Arthur Balfour, Neville Chamberlain
School with most PM alumni: Eton, 20
University with most PM alumni: Oxford, 28
First not to attend university: Devonshire
Most recent not to attend university: Major
Married in office: Sir Robert Walpole, Duke of Grafton, Lord Liverpool
Divorced in office: Duke of Grafton
Bachelors: Earl of Wilmington, Pitt the Younger, Arthur Balfour, Edward Heath
Most children: 17, Earl Grey
Richest: Lord Derby
Most in debt: Pitt the Younger

Pitt the Elder (1708–1778) became prime minister only towards the end of his life, a useful reminder that many of those who reach the top spot have first distinguished themselves in other roles – and that, at a time when a leader usually sat in the House of Lords, a vital duty would often be to champion and enforce his government's policies in the Commons.

Arriving on the scene in 1735 at the age of 27, Pitt quickly established himself as an awkward character and a firebrand off-the-cuff debater, fixing his opponents with a glaring eye and playing up the agonies he habitually suffered from gout for dramatic effect.

He set up a Peelite Whig faction to oppose Walpole, who slapped him down for his disloyalty by stripping him of the cornetcy he'd bought to join his uncle's cavalry regiment.

He wasn't afraid to make an enemy of the King either, describing George II's attachment to his native Hanover as 'despicable' because it diverted his attention from what he should be doing in England – which, in short, meant going to war.

His wasn't a lightning progress, despite his undeniable qualities. Even after Walpole left the scene in 1742, it was four years before Pitt was given the senior post of paymaster general under Henry Pelham, and he was then stuck in that job for all of nine years.

Of course he divided opinion. Here's Horace Walpole on his debating skills during an all-night sitting:

> He spoke at past one, for an hour and thirty-five minutes: there was more humour, wit, vivacity, finer language, more boldness in short, more astonishing perfections than... you can conceive.

And here's his fellow Whig politician Henry Fox:

> He is a better speaker than I am, but thank God! I have more judgement.

Pitt's fortunes rose under the premiership of the Duke of Newcastle, who took over the reins on the death of his younger brother but who – despite having served for many years as secretary of state – was totally unsuited to running a government.

Immensely rich and well connected, Newcastle was a socially awkward hypochondriac,* who would grab people by the lapels while gabbling away at them and was given to fainting fits and even public outbreaks of weeping. Making decisions wasn't his thing at all.

As Britain drifted into war with France, who could he turn to in his hour of need but the highly competent, belligerent Pitt?

The Seven Years' War

Here's how the two sides lined up at the start of a conflict spanning five continents:

- **With Britain: Prussia, Portugal and several small German states**

- **Against: France, Austria (the Holy Roman Empire), Russia, Spain and Sweden**

It started badly for Britain but, thanks to Pitt's dynamic leadership, would end in triumph.

---

* *Visiting a bed-bound Pitt in a room kept cold for his gout, Newcastle was so worried that he might catch a chill that he climbed into another bed – the pair then discussing battle tactics from under their blankets.*

The war ran from 1756 until 1763, extended beyond Europe to the Americas, India, coastal Africa and the Philippines – and drastically changed the balance of power between Britain and France.

The Byng affair

In 1756, shortly before war was officially declared, Admiral John Byng failed to relieve a besieged British garrison in a battle with the French off Minorca and returned to Gibraltar to repair his ships. For this decision he was court-martialled, found guilty of failing to 'do his utmost' and was executed by firing squad.

Pitt was among those (including the judges at Byng's trial) who had pleaded for clemency, and George II responded by sacking him from the government. This caused such a public outcry that he was given the freedom of the City of London and thirteen other towns, with demands that he should be reinstated to lead the failing war effort.

The man they called the Great Commoner was back running the show within months.

Empire is a contentious subject these days, but Pitt is the political pin-up for anyone who has a soft spot for the time when huge areas of the globe were coloured British pink.

His vision was of an unrivalled naval power, its prosperity drawn from the resources of accumulated far-flung territories around the world.

He achieved it through what we would today call a Churchillian boldness ('I am sure,' he trumpeted, 'I can save this country and nobody else can'), and by taking close control of the armed forces, raising talented young officers to commands ahead of men with greater seniority but less imagination.

Admiral Rodney, who fought with distinction in the war, later proclaimed Pitt as an example of how 'one great man, by his superior abilities, raised his drooping country from the brink of despaire to the pinnacle of glory'.

Frederick the Great of Prussia was weak at the knees: 'England has been a long time in labour but she has, at last, brought forth a man.'

Two French strongholds in North America*
were captured in 1758, while the following
year General Wolfe seized Quebec and there
were further British gains in the Caribbean,
India and West Africa. The victories were
relentless.

Under the Treaty of Paris in 1763 France
ceded to Britain:

- All of mainland North America east
  of the Mississippi River, bar New Orleans
- All their recent conquests in India and the
  East Indies
- Sovereignty over Canada, Dominica,
  Grenada, Saint Vincent and Tobago

A pittance?

By this time, however, Pitt was out of office
– and grumbling about terms that he thought
too generous to the French. The Whig-hating
George III had come to the throne and had
installed a Tory premier, Lord Bute, who
ejected his opponents in what became known
as The Massacre of the Pelham Innocents.

* One of them, Fort Duquesne, was renamed Pittsburgh.

Also rans

The Marquess of **Rockingham** is known for his enthusiasm for the turf rather than for his two brief terms as Prime Minister. His government had a good smattering of his pals from the Jockey Club; he ran his own stables; he chose the name for the classic race, the St Leger; and he was the patron of George Stubbs, whose painting of Rockingham's Whistlejacket is in the National Gallery.

His private secretary was the political author Edmund Burke, and Rockingham changed his will in order to pay Burke's debts.

The Duke of **Grafton** (a single brief term) was likewise mad on the races, and his horses won the Derby three times. His passion for women was equally intense. He lived openly with a racy mistress; divorced his wife when she conveniently ran off with the Earl of Upper Ossory; and then married again – fathering thirteen children in addition to the three he already had.

In his retirement he served as Chancellor of Cambridge University and published books and essays on religion – urging the upper classes to live more virtuously.

His reputation went south

Poor Lord North will be for ever saddled with responsibility for losing the American colonies because it happened on his watch, but his defenders might wish to point the finger at George Grenville (Pitt the Elder's brother-in-law) for starting the trouble.

Perhaps because he ran a fiscally responsible government, he thought it reasonable to impose his Stamp Act on the colonists in 1765 – thinking it was only fair that they should bear some of the costs of defeating the French in the Seven Years' War.

The Act was later repealed, but the anger would never subside. Shortly before he began his premiership, North voted in favour of a decision to impose a tea tax on the colonists. In 1773 they threw the stuff into the water at the so-called Boston Tea Party; he responded by threatening to send in frigates; in 1775 the first shots of what would become the American War of Independence were fired at Lexington and Concord; and by 1783 it was all over.

As he already knew, North's reputation was irredeemably tarnished.

Although he was yet to become prime minister (a late flourish during which he took the title Earl of Chatham, and left the Commons), Pitt's major contribution to British life was over.

He lived another ten years after resigning the premiership through ill health, his last throw of the dice being an unavailing opposition to the loss of the American colonies from the empire he had so vigorously sought to expand.

A political Mozart

Fifteen years after Pitt stepped down as prime minister his second son adopted the mantle.

Pitt the Younger (1759–1806) was a child prodigy. Like his contemporary Mozart, he trod in paternal footsteps and (before going up to Cambridge) was educated at home: his father had been sent to Eton but he wasn't prepared to put the lad through an experience which, he said, left boys 'cowed for life'.

And, again like Mozart, he developed very quickly, going on to become an MP at 21 and prime minister, ridiculously, at just 24.

His style was different, but young Pitt was as commanding a Commons presence as his father had been.* He amazed MPs with his maiden speech, which – called on to deliver out of the blue – he carried off with brazen confidence and without notes.

He turned down George III's first invitation to become prime minister because the powerful North and Fox factions had joined forces in the Commons against him, but the king promptly broke up their coalition and persuaded Pitt to step up to the plate.

Those french again

For most of his premiership Pitt doubled as chancellor of the exchequer, and at the outset he set himself the task (which he achieved) of reducing a national debt which had soared during the American War of Independence.

Unfortunately there was soon to be yet another heavy drain on his government's expenses.

---

* He was similarly brought low by gout. His doctor prescribed a bottle of port a day – a regime he followed throughout his life, probably making things worse.

In 1793, embroiled in a bloody revolution which had created a republic and guillotined a king, France declared war on Britain.

The hostilities lasted until the end of Pitt's first term of office in 1801, and no sooner had he returned to the helm three years later than Napoleon Bonaparte had made himself emperor and was busily – and devastatingly – waging war all over again.

A regent parked

The greatest threat to Pitt's long reign as prime minister lay in George III's mental health. In 1788, when he suffered the first of his bouts of madness, the obvious candidate as regent was the larger-than-life Prince of Wales, later George IV.

'Prinnie' was a supporter of Charles James Fox (who fought five general elections and lost them all), and he was itching to propel his favourite into the top seat. Fortunately for Pitt, Parliament spent months debating the issue. The king recovered his wits just before a Regency Bill was passed – and his son had to hang on for more than twenty years.

The coalitions of European monarchies Pitt forged against France lost rather too many battles for comfort, but historians generally credit him with keeping the Royal Navy in good heart* and stiffening the national resolve – although the witty cleric Sydney Smith quipped that 'at the close of every brilliant display an expedition failed or a kingdom fell'.

He died well before Old Boney, as the English half admiringly called him, had finished his long march of destruction.

A high point of his last days was Nelson's victory at Trafalgar in 1805, which led to Pitt being toasted as 'the saviour of Europe' at the lord mayor's banquet.

A low point, weeks later, was Napoleon's devastating victory over the Austrians and Russians at Austerlitz, after which a gloomy Pitt is reported to have said, 'Roll up that map of Europe: it will not be wanted these next ten years.'

* To pay for the war effort he invented income tax – intended to be a temporary measure.

Rooting out the radicals

At home, Pitt's record was tarnished by his government's ruthless pursuit of republicans and other 'radicals' it suspected of intentions to overthrow the state.

This relentless oppression, which included raids on private houses and a network of spies, their ears pricked for subversive conversations, is easily explained: the upper classes were in a blue funk about what was happening across the Channel in revolutionary France. A range of laws was introduced to stamp out dissent:

- In 1794 the suspension of habeas corpus allowed arrest and imprisonment 'on suspicion' without charge or trial
- The Treasonable Practices Act of 1795 extended the definition of 'treason' to speaking or writing
- The Seditious Meetings Act of 1795 forbade gatherings of more than 50 people without a magistrate's permission
- The Combination Acts of 1799 and 1800 prohibited societies or 'amalgamations of persons' from advocating political reform

The Wilberforce Oak

On a May day in 1787 Pitt sat under an oak*
on his Holwood estate in Kent with two other
MPs, his old friend William Grenville and a
newer one, William Wilberforce. All three
opposed slavery, and it was this meeting which
energised Wilberforce to fight for the cause in
parliament against powerful vested interests.

Pitt never lived to see the battle won. It was
during Grenville's premiership that the first
blow was struck, the Slave Trade Act of 1807
abolishing the dealing in slaves throughout the
British colonies. (He so disliked being prime
minister, and found the king so difficult to deal
with, that he resigned as soon as it was given
the royal assent, thankfully breathing 'I am
again a free man'.)

The decisive Slavery Abolition Act of 1833
would later do away with the practice of slavery
as well as the trade in it. Wilberforce witnessed
that successful conclusion to his campaign –
and died four days later.

---

* *The original tree died, but a replacement planted in 1969 stands at
the spot today.*

The *Rights of Man* author Thomas Paine, whose effigy was burned across the country, was tried for sedition in 1792 (and found guilty) but had already fled the country.

Two years later, after an initial arrest of thirty radicals, three men (Thomas Hardy, John Horne Took and John Thelwall) were tried for high treason in a celebrated case that was clearly intended to crush free speech.

Thomas Erskine, defending them, so clearly demonstrated that their opinions posed no threat to public order that – in a triumph for the rule of law, and to public rejoicing – the charges were completely thrown out.

At another time Pitt might have been able to follow his liberal instincts. He deplored slavery, was in favour of Catholic emancipation (in 1801 he resigned over it) and once even made an unsuccessful attempt at parliamentary reform.

The fearful spirit of the age had made that the work of the next generation...

' Now, gentlemen –
who will be the
first to fall? '

CHAPTER THREE

SHOT
IN THE LOBBY

Late in the afternoon of 11th May, 1812, as Prime Minister Spencer Perceval crossed a busy House of Commons lobby on his way to a debate about his handling of the Napoleonic wars, a figure emerged through the crowd, pointed a pistol at his chest from point-blank range and fired. He was pronounced dead within minutes.

The instant acclaim for his killer by swathes of a downtrodden public throws the political turbulence of the time into sharp relief. As he was bundled into a hackney coach, swarms of well-wishers surged forward to shake his hand and had to be beaten back with whips.

The law reformer and MP Samuel Romilly reported hearing 'the most savage expressions of joy and exultation', along with regrets that the attorney-general and other members of the government hadn't suffered a similar fate.

Not only was unemployment high at a time of wartime depression, but Perceval (commonly known as Little P because of his diminutive frame), had continued Pitt's repressive policy towards dissent.

Mobs had rioted when the radical MP Sir Francis Burdett was sent to the Tower of London for publishing an anti-government letter in William Cobbett's *Weekly Register*. Now Cobbett wrote from his own prison cell at Newgate (a two-year sentence for protesting against the flogging of local militiamen) that Perceval's death had 'ridded them of one whom they looked upon as the leader among those whom they thought totally bent on the destruction of their liberties'.

The authorities, fearing that an insurrection might be on the way, sent mounted troops onto the streets in readiness.

In fact the reality was more humdrum: the motive of Perceval's killer was personal rather than political.

John Bellingham was a 43-year-old Liverpool trader who had spent some five years banged up in a Russian prison over what he said was a trumped-up fraud charge.

His grievance was that the British government had failed to compensate him for his ordeal. In court he spoke as if what he had done was entirely reasonable:

> My family was ruined and myself destroyed merely because it was Mr Perceval's pleasure that justice should not be granted; sheltering himself behind the imagined security of his station, and trampling upon law and right in the belief that no retribution could reach him. I demand only my right, and not a favour; I demand what is the birthright and privilege of every Englishman.

After he was hanged,* a public subscription was raised for his wife and children.

---

* *Bellingham's skull is on display in the museum of St Bartholomew's Hospital at Smithfield, London, where his body was dissected.*

Rough and tumble

Although Perceval's murder has been the only assassination of a British prime minister, there have – as we shall shortly see – been a few near misses. More common, through the ages, have been rowdy incidents and displays of public discontent.

– Nobody likes paying tax, but new levies brought in by Walpole in 1733 sparked the so-called Excise Crisis. His effigy was burned in the streets, and when a mob threatened him outside the Commons, Henry Pelham ushered Walpole into a narrow passage leading to Alice's coffee house, drew his sword and demanded: 'Now, gentlemen – who will be the first to fall?' Luckily there were no takers.

– The cider tax of 1763 was part of the reason for Lord Bute's unpopularity,* though being a Scot didn't help and a rumoured relationship with Augusta, Princess of Wales, only made things worse.

---

* But he was quite a looker and was said to have 'the best legs in London'.

– The windows of his London house were smashed, and several years later he and Augusta were still being burned in effigy – she sometimes represented as a petticoat, he (since his first name was John and his surname was pronounced 'boot') by a jackboot.

– Very early in his first premiership, when Pitt the Younger was granted the Freedom of the City of London, his coach was pulled home not by horses but (as a mark of respect) by City gentlemen themselves. They made the mistake of passing a club frequented by the rival Whig party, and Pitt had to be defended from thugs who tried to assault him.

– Lord Goderich, some years before he became Prime Minister, angered the public because of his support for the Corn Laws. In 1815 a mob attacked his London house while he was away, destroying pictures and furniture. His loyal butler, calamitously, fired a shot which killed an innocent bystander. Goderich broke down in tears while reporting this to the Commons, and was ever afterwards known as The Blubberer.

– Even national heroes can lose their sheen. The Duke of Wellington, Boney's scourge, was much more successful as a soldier than as a politician, and in 1830 his opposition to reform brought about a typical public response: he was hanged in effigy and his house was stoned.

Believe it or not, but some say he was dubbed the Iron Duke because of the protective shutters he put up over his windows in response.

The wrong man?

Was Prime Minister Robert Peel the intended target when his private secretary Edward Drummond was shot in the back on his way to Downing Street on a January day in 1843?

His assailant, a 30-year-old Glaswegian wood turner called Daniel M'Naughten,* had apparently been stalking Peel for days, yet for some reason he chose the wrong man when it came to pulling the trigger.

* *Pronounced McNaughton. He was overpowered by a member of the Metropolitan Police Force which Peel had set up when Home Secretary back in 1829.*

Drummond was able to walk away from the scene, and the bullet was successfully removed, but complications set in after he was bled with leeches by his doctors, and he died a few days later.

At his trial, the argument offered in M'Naughten's defence was that he was suffering from delusions. A self-taught man with radical leanings, he insisted that he was being followed by Tory spies.

'They follow, persecute me wherever I go,' he said, 'and have entirely destroyed my peace of mind.'

The jury's verdict of not guilty on the grounds of insanity provoked a public outcry, with the House of Lords questioning the judges and Queen Victoria writing to Peel to express her concern.

The upshot was that the twelve judges of the Court of Common Pleas were asked to give their ruling on the case, and a new definition of criminal insanity was enshrined in law as the M'Naughten Rules.

Duelling

As if the threat from a would-be assassin wasn't enough, two prime ministers and one future occupant of 10 Downing Street risked their lives by duelling.

In May 1798 George Tierney MP, the treasurer of the Navy, took umbrage at a statement by the premier, William Pitt the Younger, which he regarded as a slur on his personal courage and patriotism. He threw down a challenge, and the two duly exchanged shots on Putney Common. Some thought it unfair that the skinny Pitt had an advantage over his portly (and therefore easier to hit) adversary – both missed – but a greater criticism was that it happened on a Sunday.

During the Duke of Portland's premiership the minister for war, Lord Castlereagh, learned that the foreign secretary, George Canning, had been plotting against him. He sent a challenging letter, but Canning said he would rather fight than read it. Castlereagh had fought a duel over a woman as a young man, but Canning had never fired a pistol in his life: before their confrontation on Putney Heath in September 1809 he wrote his will and a farewell letter to his wife.

Their first shots having missed, they were called together by their seconds but failed to settle their differences. Canning's second shot deflected off a coat button, while Castlereagh's inflicted a slight wound on his opponent's thigh. Brilliant though he was, Canning was thought to have acted recklessly in fighting the duel. This hampered his career, and he served as prime minister only for the last few months of his life.

The Duke of Wellington had once been firmly opposed to Catholic Emancipation, but during his first premiership he changed his mind and introduced a Catholic Relief Bill. This incensed the Earl of Winchelsea, a fervent Protestant, who accused him of carrying on 'his insidious designs for the infringements of our liberties and the introduction of Popery into every department of the State'. This was too much for Wellington, who issued a challenge, and in March 1829 the pair took themselves off to Battersea Fields ('Among the cabbages,' reported the *Morning Herald*) to see justice done. The duke shot first and missed, after which the earl – who clearly didn't dare be the man to kill a national hero – discharged his pistol in the air. He then offered an apology and the Duke accepted it. *Honour satisfied!*

Grand awakening

The most deadly attack against a British prime minister targeted the Conservative Party conference at Brighton in October 1984.

A few weeks earlier the Provisional IRA volunteer Patrick Magee had checked in to the Grand Hotel on the seafront and planted a 9kg (20lb) time bomb under the bath in his room on the seventh floor. It was directly above the first floor suite in which the Prime Minister, Margaret Thatcher, would be staying with her husband Denis when the Tories came to town.

The bomb exploded at 2.54am, and such was its force that a large central section of the hotel collapsed into the basement. Five people were killed in the blast, including the MP Sir Anthony Berry, and more than thirty others were injured – some of them left with permanent disabilities.

Thatcher was still up, working on her speech for the opening of the conference later that morning. Although the bathroom was badly damaged, her other rooms were untouched.

The IRA issued a statement rehearsing its grievances against the government and ending with a chilling warning: 'Today we were unlucky, but remember we only have to be lucky once. You will have to be lucky always.'

Thatcher's response was typically bullish. She declared business as usual (the conference would go ahead), spoke of the attack as an outrage and gave a defiant message in return: 'All attempts to destroy democracy by terrorism will fail.'

The bombing coincided with a miners' strike against a mass closure of pits and, in a faint echo of the shocking response to Perceval's assassination, there were guarded murmurs of support for the IRA action. The overwhelming reaction, though, was admiration for the prime minister's Churchillian courage, and her popularity ratings soared.

Magee was given eight life sentences but was released after fourteen years (a government spokesman pronounced it 'hard to swallow') as part of the Good Friday Agreement devised to bring peace to Northern Ireland.

Margaret Thatcher was (of course) back at the Grand Hotel to make a speech at its reopening* in August 1986, and the event was also marked by a low pass from the south by Concorde, the British-French supersonic passenger airliner.

Downing Street mortar

The IRA got unlucky again on the morning of February 7th, 1991, when it fired three home-made mortar shells at no. 10 Downing Street from a van parked in the street nearby.

Thatcher was again the target when the plan was first hatched, but John Major had since become prime minister. Now he and his entire cabinet (at a pre-publicised meeting to discuss the Gulf War) were the intended victims.

Months before the attack two IRA members had bought a Ford Transit van, cut a hole in its roof, primed the shells with plastic explosive Semtex and rented a lock-up garage where this deadly cargo awaited the chosen moment.

---

* *The renovations were so extensive that the hotel's star rating rose from 4 to 5.*

On the day itself the driver approached the area in a snowstorm, left his van at the junction of Whitehall and Horse Guards Avenue and made off on a motorbike. The shells were launched a little after ten o'clock – followed by the explosion of a pre-set incendiary device to set the van ablaze and destroy any evidence.

Two of the shells landed on Mountbatten Green, near the Foreign and Commonwealth Office, but the third exploded in the no. 10 garden, scorching the brickwork, breaking windows and creating a crater several feet deep.

Murdered MPs

Although only one prime minister has been assassinated, seven other MPs have been murdered.

By Irish Republicans: Lord Frederick Cavendish (1882); Sir Henry Wilson (1922); Airey Neave (1979); Rev Robert Bradford (1981); Sir Anthony Berry (1984); Ian Gow (1990).

By a white supremacist: Jo Cox (2016).

Major and his colleagues felt the blast, but the bomb-proof netting at the windows saved them from injury – and only four people, including two police officers, were slightly hurt.

Peter Gurney, an explosives expert for the Metropolitan Police, struck an almost gushing note of admiration when he described the IRA assault to the media.

> It was a remarkably good aim if you consider that the bomb was fired 250 yards [230m] with no direct line of sight. Technically it was quite brilliant, and I'm sure that many army crews, if given a similar task, would be very pleased to drop a bomb that close.
> You've got to park the launch vehicle in an area which is guarded by armed men and you've got less than a minute to do it. I was very, very surprised at how good it was. If the angle of fire had been moved about five or ten degrees, then those bombs would actually have impacted on no. 10.

Major himself was less complimentary: 'It's about time they learned that democracies cannot be intimidated by terrorism, and we treat them with contempt.'

The reality, as ever, was rather more nuanced. It was discovered years later that Margaret Thatcher had already sanctioned the opening of secret talks between her officials and the IRA leadership.

Although peace would later come to Ireland, however, the time when a prime minister's safety could be taken for granted had long since passed.

' They are mad,
they are mad! '

CHAPTER FOUR

SHAKING THE FOUNDATIONS

For a statesman who left an indelible mark on his country's constitution it's an oddity that Earl Grey should be best known to the general public for the bergamot-infused tea he took to drinking on his Northumberland estate (the local lime-rich water produced an unsavoury brew) and which his wife popularised when entertaining on the London scene.

This was the man, after all, who averted the genuine threat of an English Revolution by driving through the Great Reform Bill of 1832 – overhauling a parliamentary system unfairly skewed in favour of grandees like himself.

The comeback king

Earl Grey (1764–1845) was a reformer from his youth, entering Parliament as a Whig at the age of 22 and making an immediate impression* with a fiery attack on Pitt the Younger in his maiden speech.

In 1806 he was appointed First Lord of the Admiralty in a coalition known as the Ministry of All the Talents, and within months he was both foreign secretary and leader of the Whigs.

That seemed to be the high point of his career. He resigned in 1807 when George III demanded that all his ministers sign a pledge against the cause of Catholic Emancipation. The Tories resumed power, and the Whigs were cast into the political wilderness for all of 23 years – until Grey's sudden comeback as prime minister in 1830 at the age of 66.

*Lord Byron loved his 'patrician thoroughbred look' – as did the wayward Georgiana, Duchess of Devonshire, who bore him a daughter and (threatened by the Duke with divorce) gave her to Grey's parents to bring up as their own. When he was 30, Grey married the 18-year-old Mary Ponsonby, and they went on to have 15 children.

However much a succession of Tory premiers turned a blind eye to it (Liverpool proudly insisted that 'the landed interest is the stamina of the country'), the electoral system was plainly, and unsustainably, corrupt.

The most glaring injustice was that while essentially fake rural boroughs sent two MPs each to Parliament – sparsely populated Cornwall supplied 44 of them – cities such as Manchester and Birmingham, mushrooming in response to the industrial revolution, had no representation at all.

Grey had first attempted to push reform through Parliament back in the 1790s, only to suffer two crushing defeats, but a series of violent disturbances at last frightened the authorities into treating it seriously.

- **The destruction of machinery by Luddites, who feared that mechanisation threatened their livelihoods, was a sign of the working classes refusing to be cowed. Millowners responded by shooting protesters, and an Act of 1812 made 'frame-breaking' a capital offence.**

- In 1819 a mass protest in Manchester over the lack of parliamentary reform was put down by a vicious sabre-wielding charge by the 15th Hussars which left more than a dozen people dead and hundreds injured.*

- Threatening letters from a fictional Captain Swing were sent to authority figures during the summer of 1830, when depressed agricultural workers went on the rampage, breaking threshing machines, burning barns and even maiming cattle in what were known as the Swing Riots.

The authorities responded with their usual severity, but something had to change.

Teamwork

Getting his legislation through the House of Lords was Grey's biggest headache, but he was a canny operator. Having waited more than twenty years for this chance, he wasn't going to let it slip through his fingers.

---

* As it took place at St Peter's Field and occurred four years after the Battle of Waterloo, this bloody event became known as the Peterloo Massacre.

He was himself a reluctant member of the upper chamber, and had reacted angrily when his father accepted a peerage. On the old man's death in 1807 Grey duly moved to the Lords, where making a speech (he lamented in a letter to his wife) was 'like speaking in a vault by a sepulchral light to the dead'.

Royal assent

The death of George IV in 1830, and the accession of his brother as William IV, was a shot in the arm for Grey's reforms.

The mutual loathing between George and Queen Caroline had been played out as public entertainment: he refused to have her attend his coronation, and when she tried to force her way into Westminster Abbey bayonets were held under her chin and the door was slammed in her face.

The Tories at first supported George's wish for a divorce, but the Whigs under Grey opposed it – to the King's fury. William had no such hostility towards him, and when Wellington pronounced against electoral reform in the Lords, the King immediately sent for Grey.

Taking a softly, softly approach to his reforms, he brought into his cabinet landowners of such wealth that no previous government (or such was his claim) could match them for the number of acres they owned.

No fewer than four of them would be among the country's next six prime ministers.

- William Lamb, later Lord Melbourne, had a turbulent emotional life in his early years. His wife Caroline made no secret of her dramatic affair with the poet Byron, while he himself had scandalous relationships with various married women and twice appeared in divorce suits.

- Who would have guessed that Melbourne would develop from careless debauchee into the young Queen Victoria's wise counsellor?

- John Russell,* an ardent reformer, was Grey's leading representative in the Commons (he would be created an earl much later) and he eagerly threw himself into the challenge.

---

* Since he was a short man and his first wife had been recently bereaved, wits dubbed him 'the widow's mite'.

One of his strengths was that he seemed not to care what people thought of him. Gladstone would later say that 'no man ever led the House of Commons with a more many-sided activity or more indomitable pluck'.

During his two terms as prime minister he was to continue his reforming zeal, with legislation covering public health and working conditions.

- **Although Edward Stanley (later Lord Derby) was another of Grey's advocates in the Commons, he later switched from the Whigs to the Conservatives.**

That, he insisted (and demonstrated), was no bar to progressive policies: 'We live in an age of constant progress, moral, social and political,' he told the Lords at the launch of his second premiership (he notched up three, all of them brief). 'Our constitution itself is the result of a series of perpetual changes.'

In his third term of office – 34 years after Gray's landmark legislation – Derby would introduce the Second Reform Bill, extending the franchise further.

PM fact file 3

Tallest: Salisbury, 1.93m (6ft 4in)
Shortest: Perceval, 1.62m (5ft 4in)
First not from landed gentry: Addington
   (Later created Lord Sidmouth)
Last to govern from the Lords: Salisbury
Never a minister before becoming PM: 4
   Rockingham, MacDonald, Blair, Cameron
Never been the subject of a biography:
   Wilmington
**Descended from the Crown through royal
   mistresses:** Grafton, Cameron*
Facial hair: Disraeli, goatee; Salisbury, full set
Jewish birth: Disraeli
Bilingual: Lloyd George (Welsh & English)
Roman Catholic: Blair (after leaving office)
Permanent injuries from accidents:
   Gladstone lost part of finger in firearm
   accident
   Macmillan, a limp and damaged hand from
   WWI wounds
   Brown, partially blind from rugby accident
Nobel prize: Winston Churchill (for Literature)
Most decorated: Winston Churchill,
   38 UK orders, decorations and medals; 13
   from other states

** Grafton from Charles II and Barbara Villiers; Cameron from
William IV and Dorothea Jordan.*

An aloof, somewhat unbending character, he was nevertheless generous to the workers on his estates, sending his own doctor to look after the sick and sprinkling cash to prevent families being forced in the workhouse.

- **Lord Palmerston, always a maverick, always quarrelsome (Victoria yoked him with Russell as 'those two dreadful old men'), brought an irrepressible vigour to Gray's campaign.**

Very much his own man – and widely admired for it – he switched almost carelessly between the Whigs and the Conservatives before becoming the first Liberal prime minister.

Foreign affairs was his speciality. Always giving the impression of not taking anything too seriously, he typically brought his wit to bear on an obscure diplomatic tussle between Denmark and Germany:

> Only three people have ever really understood the Schleswig-Holstein business – the Prince Consort who is dead, a German professor who has gone mad and I, who have forgotten all about it.

After many years as secretary at war and foreign secretary, Palmerston would become prime minister during the Crimean War and, with a short break, would occupy the post for more than nine years.

Taming the Lords

These, then, were some of the big guns Grey brought to bear in his attempt to overturn an electoral system not fit for purpose.

The shock experienced in the Commons when Russell introduced the first version of his reform bill was vividly described by John Cam Hobhouse,* then Gray's secretary at war:

> Never shall I forget the astonishment of my neighbours as he developed his plan. Indeed, all the House seemed perfectly astounded; and when he read the long list of the boroughs to be either wholly or partially disfranchised there was a sort of wild ironical laughter. Baring Wall [MP] turned to me, said, 'They are mad, they are mad!'

---

* Best known today as a friend of Lord Byron.

The shake-up was, indeed, more extensive than many thought credible, its declared purpose being 'to take effectual Measures for correcting divers Abuses that have long prevailed in the Choice of Members to serve in the Commons House of Parliament'.

- Out went more than 50 rotten, pocket and so-called pot-walloper boroughs – those in which men could vote if they had a hearth big enough to boil a large pot of water

- Thirty boroughs sending two MPs to Parliament had their allotment cut to one

- Forty-two new boroughs were created, 22 of them electing two MPs and 20 with a single representative

- The shire counties were split into divisions, each with its own MP

The bill passed by one vote and was defeated on a wrecking amendment a month later.

Unfazed, Gray immediately called a general election – and won it by a landslide.

A second version of the bill passed successfully through the Commons but was promptly thrown out by the Lords.

Cue riots throughout the land! The Lords Spiritual had voted against the bill, and in Bristol protesters destroyed the Bishop's palace and the lord mayor's mansion in a three-day spree which also saw the release of prisoners from local gaols.

There were violent outbreaks in Dorset and Somerset, while in the Midlands a mob set fire to Nottingham Castle (home of the Duke of Newcastle) and damaged Lord Middleton's Wollaton Hall.

Gamesmanship

Grey now coolly used his considerable skills to engineer eventual victory. After driving a third bill through the lower house, he asked the King to stack the Lords with dozens of new, reform-friendly peers – and when that request was (perhaps predictably) refused, Grey resigned, confidently awaiting the next stage of the drama.

William's response was to recall the Iron Duke, but in the turmoil of the time Wellington found himself unable to form a government.

During a period of heady political agitation known as the Days of May, protesters sought to hit the authorities where it hurt – in their pockets. They urged a run on the banks (signs appeared in London reading 'Stop the Duke – Go for Gold'), and within days £1.8 million, or about a quarter of the Bank of England's gold reserves, had been withdrawn.

The newly formed National Political Union sent a petition to the Commons demanding that it cut off government funding until the Lords came to heel, while at mass meetings there were calls for the abolition of the nobility and the monarchy.

The King had little choice but to reinstate Grey and let him have his new peers after all.

At this point Wellington caved in. No new peers were necessary, because he would whip his Tories into line to abstain from voting. The Great Reform Bill narrowly became law.

'Please, sir...'

Lord Grey added to his liberal reputation in 1833, the Slavery Abolition Act banning the practice throughout the Empire and the Factory Act improving conditions for children working in factories.

The Poor Law Amendment Act, passed shortly before he retired a year later, had a very different reception. Charles Dickens's *Oliver Twist* highlights the cruelty of workhouses established to sort the undeserving from the deserving poor, his young hero punished for wanting more to eat.

Up in flames

You can probably guess a common reaction when the Houses of Parliament burned down in 1834 – a massive conflagration that was captured in oils by Turner, Constable and several other artists.

The writer Thomas Carlyle, who stood in the vast watching crowd, reported that 'a man sorry I did not anywhere see', one suggestion being that it was 'a judgement for the Poor Law Bill'.

Little by little

Grey of course had no thoughts about one man, one vote – let alone votes for women. His reform package increased the suffrage from around 400,000 to 650,000, or about a fifth of the adult male population, and he resigned soon afterwards, proud of a job well done.

However modest it may have been by today's standards, his Great Reform Bill changed the political landscape for ever. The historian G.M. Trevelyan compared its impact with that of the Glorious Revolution.

In our domestic history 1832 is the next great landmark after 1688. It saved the land from revolution and civil strife, and made possible the quiet progress of the Victorian era...

A star who fell to earth

Robert Peel (1788–1850) provides a classic example of a principled politician having to choose when to stick and when to twist in challenging times – even if, in his case, the choice gives you a lasting reputation as the man who destroyed his own party.

First the dutiful schoolboy, a comrade of Lord Byron at Harrow but without, as the poet later said, his tendency to get into scrapes. Next the brilliant scholar, the first to be awarded a double first at Oxford. Then, at just 22, an MP giving the best maiden speech since Pitt the Younger.

Peel would go on to become a great home secretary, creating the Metropolitan Police and reforming the criminal law codes, before twice serving as prime minister.

Orange Peel
At 24 his mentor, the Duke of Wellington, appointed him secretary for Ireland, in which role he argued so fervently against Catholic emancipation that the Irish nationalist leader Daniel O'Connell called him Orange Peel. (They agreed to fight a duel, but O'Connell was detained in London at the time.)

Now fast forward twelve years to 1829, with O'Connell voted in as an MP (although not allowed to sit in parliament) and Ireland on the verge of a religious civil war. With public sentiment and the Whig opposition in favour of a more liberal policy, Wellington and Peel surrendered, their Roman Catholic Relief Act removing most restrictions on Catholics taking part in public life.

They were, of course, regarded as traitors by many staunch Protestants: the Duchess of Richmond displayed stuffed rats named Peel and Wellington in her drawing room.

Chartism

Grey's electoral reforms only stirred working class agitation for a more extensive spread of the franchise. The Chartists, a flourishing organisation during Peel's second term, made six demands,* among them universal male suffrage, secret ballots and payment for MPs.

Peel resisted these calls, but his success in righting an economy which had been in the doldrums since the Napoleonic Wars – cutting indirect taxes along the way – helped defuse public anger.

* Only one of them, annual elections, was never introduced in the years to come.

The price of bread

In the Tamworth Manifesto – a personal political creed, issued in his Staffordshire constituency when first becoming prime minister – Peel accepted Gray's Reform Act as 'final and irrevocable' and pledged that the Conservatives would carry out a 'careful' review of civil and ecclesiastical institutions.

Few can have imagined that this reasonable flexibility would extend to repealing the Corn Laws, hated by the lower classes since being introduced in 1815.

The laws fixed punitive tariffs on the imports of grain from overseas, so keeping prices high for the benefit of British landowners. This of course meant higher food prices for the consumer – and with a reduction in disposable income it had a knock-on effect on many businesses, too.

Peel, who claimed to have read 'all that has been written by the gravest authorities on political economy on the subject of rent, wages, taxes, tithes,' steadfastly voted against repeal year after year from 1837.

What changed his mind was a dreadful harvest in the autumn of 1845 and the onset of the Great Famine in Ireland.

As the potato crop failed, a million people in Ireland would perish from starvation and disease, with a million more forced to emigrate.

Peel knew what he must do. With the Whigs in support, but two thirds of his own party against him, he forced through the repeal of the Corn Laws – and immediately stepped down.

In his resignation speech he admitted that he would always be despised by those whose pockets he had hit, but he hoped that many others would think of him more kindly.

It may be that I shall leave a name sometimes remembered with expressions of goodwill in the abode of those whose lot it is to labour, and to earn their daily bread by the sweat of their brow, when they shall recruit their exhausted strength with abundant and untaxed food, the sweeter because it is no longer leavened by a sense of injustice.

Peel's moral stand split his party. The 'Peelite' wing joined the Whigs to form the Liberal Party under Palmerston and Gladstone, while Derby and Disraeli became the leaders of the new Conservative Party.

> ⁶ He has not a single
> redeeming defect. ⁹

CHAPTER FIVE

DIZZY V THE PEOPLE'S WILLIAM

P olitical skirmishes in their most brutal manifestations display all the bruising cut-and-thrust of a boxing match, and there were no more relentlessly punishing slugfests in the Victorian arena than the seemingly endless series of bouts between Disraeli (in the Conservative corner) and Gladstone (champion of the Liberals).

These two heavyweights swung proverbial punches at one another for three decades – and so successfully that for years on end nobody else could get a look in. What added extra spice to the rivalry was the fact that they simply couldn't stand the sight of one another.

Their names live on

Here are a few prime minister namesakes, in the order of their premierships.

Wilmington: Cities in US states of Delaware and North Carolina

Rockingham: Numerous cities in USA, including North Carolina

Pitt the Elder: Pittsburgh Pennsylvania

Portland: Street names in London; the Portland Vase in the British Museum

Liverpool: Liverpool Street (and Station) in London

Wellington: capital of New Zealand; a school; a boot; Wellingtonia tree; beef Wellington

Grey: Earl Grey tea; a college at Durham University

Melbourne: capital of state of Victoria, Australia

Palmerston: Lord Palmerston pub, London

Gladstone: The Gladstone bag

Rosebery: Streets and buildings in London

Salisbury: (Now Harare) Capital of Southern Rhodesia (now Zimbabwe)

Eden: Anthony Eden black homburg hat

Churchill: a cigar; a tank; ships; a steam train; a Cambridge college; a range in the Rocky mountains; various towns, parks and lakes in Canada and Australia

98

Disraeli (1804–1881) was known to friends and foes alike as Dizzy – it captured the zing of his personality. Gladstone (1809–1898) was sometimes The People's William because of his popularity among the working classes, but more often (a tag he preferred) the Grand Old Man, or GOM. Disraeli said it stood for God's Only Mistake!

Here, to be going along with, are a couple more of the insults they traded:

> Disraeli: 'That unprincipled maniac Gladstone – extraordinary mixture of envy, vindictiveness, hypocrisy and superstition.'

> Gladstone: 'The Tory party had principles by which it would and did stand, for bad and for good. All this Dizzy destroyed.'

Chalk and cheese

Aside from their political differences, the two men were far apart in both their backgrounds and their temperaments. They were on course for a collision from the start.

Gladstone had the conventional pedigree of an Eton and Oxford education. Declining the prompting of his deeply religious father to enter the priesthood, he became an MP at the age of 22 and soon caught the eye of Robert Peel, for whom he later became President of the Board of Trade.

This early Gladstone was not only a Tory, but a reactionary one to boot. As president of the Oxford Union he made a speech against Grey's Great Reform Bill, and he both defended his father's ownership of slaves in the West Indies and advocated a ruthless suppression of dissent by Catholics in Ireland.

Although his political views soon changed, what remained constant throughout his career was a moral and deeply Christian earnestness.

The witty Disraeli again, pricking what he saw as his insufferable piety: 'He has not a single redeeming defect.'

Disraeli was the great outsider – rising to the top of what he called 'the greasy pole' despite the odds being heavily stacked against him.

His educational background? Higham High School, Walthamstow. Money? None – or worse, because as a young man he gambled on shares in mining companies and lost; then launched a newspaper he hoped would rival *The Times* and it flopped.

The Jewish question

But his greatest handicap was being Jewish. His grandfather had emigrated from Italy to London in 1748 and made his money from selling imported straw hats. His father, Isaac D'Israeli (a man of letters, whose *Curiosities of Literature* was published in six volumes between 1791 and 1834) renounced Judaism and had the young Benjamin christened in the Church of England at the age of 12.

That was a vital decision, because Jews still suffered many restrictions in Britain, and it wasn't until 1858 that the country would see its first Jewish MP.

Disraeli dropped the apostrophe in his name (his opponents would sometimes reinstate it to stress his origins) and at the age of 28 set about getting himself elected to parliament.

Anti-semitism would dog him all his political life, even from Conservatives. Lord Derby three times appointed him chancellor of the exchequer, yet he relished reading aloud to chuckling friends at his club a letter describing him as 'that nasty, oily, slimy Jew'.

During the boisterousness of an election campaign the prejudice was often extreme. Strips of bacon were stuck on poles and waved in his face to cries of 'Shylock!'

He stood three times in Wycombe as an 'independent radical' and then – ever the pragmatist – switched to the Conservatives. At his fifth attempt, in 1837, he was at last an MP.

Ruffled shirts and ringlets

Disraeli was an outrageous dandy. As a young man his hair hung in cascades of ringlets, and he sported ruffled shirts, coloured waistcoats and jewellery.

A man about town, he had a notorious affair with Henrietta Sykes, a baronet's wife who he then shared with his patron, Lord Lyndhurst.

> 'When I want to read a novel
> I write one.'
>
> *Benjamin Disraeli*

A happy marriage to a wealthy widow twelve years his senior calmed those fires, but he was always an exotic in the Westminster sphere.

Even what we might call his hobby had a dashing flavour. He wrote a flurry of frothy romantic novels in the years before he got into parliament – *Henrietta Temple* daringly told the story of his fling with the baronet's wife – and then published five with social and political themes in the fallow years when he was out of power:

> *Coningsby* 1844
> *Sybil* 1845
> *Tancred* 1847
> *Lothar* 1868
> *Endymion* 1880

Critics have panned their creaking plots and unconvincing dialogue (Trollope called the books 'pasteboard'), but the best have a vitality which has kept them in print ever since.

Disraeli, who is today regarded as the founder of One-nation Conservatism, tackles the subject in *Sybil*, with Britain seen as divided into 'two nations between whom there is no intercourse and no sympathy; who are as ignorant of each other's habits, thoughts and feelings, as if they were dwellers in different zones, or inhabitants of different planets: the rich and the poor'.

Ladies of the night

Gladstone wrote his first book in his twenties, but it was about as far from a racy Disraeli novel as you could get. Its title, *The State in its Relations with the Church*, probably tells you as much as you want to know: his ideas were regarded as a medieval throwback, and he confessed later that 'I found myself the last man on a sinking ship'.

Fluent in Latin, Greek and several modern European languages, he debated with German theologians in their own language and wrote the controversial *Studies on Homer and the Homeric Age* which, among much else, analysed the way Homeric language related to colours.

His strangest hobby, which he practised even after he became prime minister, was to pace the London streets by night (while his wife was back home in Wales) looking for prostitutes he could save from their trade.

Sometimes he worked with charities for fallen women, but increasingly it was a lone patrol in which, as he frankly admitted, he 'courted evil' by exposing himself to temptation. He then went back to his rooms and flagellated himself.

A reader's digest

On a February day in 1892 the 79-year-old Gladstone travelled to Osborne on the Isle of Wight for the formal hand-kissing ceremony with the Queen to mark his becoming prime minister (for the third time) – and on the long journey he read *Treasure Island*.

We know this because he kept a meticulous record of when and where he read* all the 20,000 books he browsed during his long life. He also enjoyed rearranging his library, which eventually totalled 30,000 volumes.

* And re-read – in the case of the *Iliad*, 36 times.

The evidence suggests that this steadfastly Christian, carnally tormented man managed to survive his ordeals unblemished, but his diaries show that he read pornography, including Restoration verse and bawdy French fables, while after visiting women who turned him on sexually he hymned their attractions in heated (no doubt immaculate) Italian.

Seconds out

The first political bout between this strikingly mismatched couple took place on a night in December 1852, with searing flashes from a thunderstorm lighting up the Commons chamber.

Disraeli had begun his career in a decidedly rickety fashion, having his maiden speech ridiculed and being turned down by Peel for a government post. By this time, though, he had helped destroy Peel's career over the repeal of the Corn Laws and was serving under Derby as chancellor of the exchequer.

He was out of his depth, and Gladstone, in a brilliant speech, destroyed his budget.

Derby's government fell, and when Aberdeen became prime minister he knew where to look for his new chancellor.

First blood to Gladstone!

But the quick-footed Disraeli was an awkward opponent to back against the ropes. He rode the blows and came back twice more to take up his former job under Derby.

On the last occasion, in 1867, he pulled a trick which stung his rival to the core. Gladstone had been Lord Russell's man in the lower chamber in the previous administration, and had failed in an attempt to bring in a new reform bill.

Bang! Out of the blue Disraeli piloted what became known as the Second Reform Act through the Commons, doubling the number of adult males eligible to vote and giving the franchise to members of the urban working class for the first time. Derby died in early 1868, and the wily Dizzy stepped up to become prime minister.

Gladstone on the deck!

The preacher and the flirt

Beneath the black mourning garb of her long widowhood Queen Victoria was a woman susceptible to male flattery, and it shouldn't surprise us that she took a shine to the practised charms of Disraeli while resenting the stiff preachiness of Gladstone who, she complained, 'speaks to me as if I were a public meeting'.

She had little sympathy for Gladstone's social reforms, and she was seriously irked by his suggestion that she should come out of her self-imposed seclusion and show the face of the royal family in public.

Disraeli, by contrast, was her favourite prime minister. He was 'peculiar', she told her daughter Vicky, but 'full of poetry, romance and chivalry. When he knelt down to kiss my hand, he said "In loving loyalty and faith".'

While Gladstone delivered verbal sermons, the smarmy Dizzy wrote her gossipy letters which she thought were just like his novels. He called her the Faerie Queen, and let her believe that he would be guided by her 'rare and choice experience' in the affairs of state rather than the demands of parliament.

She created him Earl of Beaconsfield in 1876, and he went one better a year later by persuading parliament to give her the title Empress of India. The Liberals thought that this smacked of absolutism (Gladstone ridiculed it),  but a delighted monarch turned up to open parliament in person for the first time since Albert's death.

She had regularly given him flowers, and when he died the Queen sent a wreath of primroses,* his favourite, with the words 'a tribute of affectionate regard'.

Lady Randolph Churchill has left us the best explanation of why the Queen felt as she did about the two men: 'When I left the dining room after sitting next to Gladstone I thought he was the cleverest man in England, but when I sat next to Disraeli I left feeling that I was the cleverest woman.'

---

* *Winston Churchill's father, Lord Randolph, founded the Primrose League after Disraeli's death. Designed to promote the Conservative cause, it soon had more than a million members, finally disbanding in 2004.*

The pub vote

Disraeli's first spell as prime minister lasted for just ten months. At the 1868 general election the Liberals benefited from the extended franchise he had so triumphantly introduced, and Gladstone began the first of his four terms in office.

His stated objectives were 'education, economy and reform', and he got quite a lot done in those five years.

- The Irish Church Act disestablished the Church of Ireland

- The Landlord and Tenant Act gave Irish tenants protection against landlords

- The Elementary Education Act gave England a new system of primary schools

- The Trade Union Act made unions legal, although picketing was banned under separate legislation

- The Ballot Act established secret ballots for local and general elections

Gladstone also reduced the national debt and cut income tax, but his mistake, from an electoral point of view, was to introduce a Licensing Act which restricted pub opening hours and regulated the content of beer.

When he lost the next general election he was in no doubt as to the reason: 'We have been borne down in a torrent of gin and beer.'

fighting fit

Military matters weren't generally a priority for Gladstone but, recognising that German success in the Franco-Prussian War of 1870–71 was based on the professionalism of its soldiery, he had his secretary of state for war, Edward Cardwell, instigate reforms to bring both efficiency and democracy to the British Army.

Out went flogging, bounty money for recruits and the purchase of commissions by wealthy incompetents – a prime example of the Old Boy network being Lord Cardigan's splashing out for a commission during the Crimean War and then conducting the disastrous Charge of the Light Brigade.

Dead and alive

Now it was Disraeli's turn again, and he would have six years to make his mark. Here are a few of his domestic reforms:

- **The Public Health Act, which modernised sanitary codes throughout the country**

- **Acts which allowed peaceful picketing, protected workers in factories and allowed workers to sue their employers in the civil courts if they broke legal contracts**

- **An Act making inexpensive loans available to towns and cities in order to build working-class housing**

These were genuine achievements, but Disraeli largely left them to his underlings. He was 69, his health already ailing, when he resumed the premiership (he lacked Gladstone's remarkable stamina), and a couple of years later he took himself off to the Lords to govern at a distance.

It was a reluctant move, but he tried to make the best of it: 'I am dead,' he joked, 'but in the Elysian fields.'

In these last years of his life he was less concerned with social improvements than on extending Britain's influence in the world.

Two years before contriving the grandification of Victoria as Empress of India, Disraeli had – without the sanction of Parliament – arranged to buy the nation a 44 per cent share in the Suez Canal from the Khedive of Egypt.

This turned out to be a profitable investment, although it would have consequences (*see page 150*) much later.

A bout in the Balkans

His last major scrap with Gladstone came over atrocities inflicted on Christian communities in Bulgaria by the Turks.

- Gladstone took an uncompromising moral view and denounced the blood-letting in a best-selling pamphlet.

- Disraeli, conscious that the Turks were a bulwark against Russian aggression, adopted a neutral stance during the Russo-Turkish War.

When Disraeli returned from the Congress of Berlin, where the dispute was settled, he was regarded by many as a hero.

Who, he asked, was better to represent the nation: himself or – a furious swipe at the GOM – 'a sophistical rhetorician, inebriated with the exuberance of his own verbosity, and gifted with an egotistical imagination that can at all times command an interminable and inconsistent series of arguments to malign an opponent and to glorify himself?'

On the road

All politicians expect to go on the stump these days, but the first organised meet-the-people tour was organised by the Earl of Rosebery on Gladstone's behalf in the period leading up to the 1880 general election.

During the Midlothian Campaign (named after his Scottish constituency) he drew huge crowds and – in widely reported speeches that lasted for hours at a time – accused Disraeli of using international tensions to distract the public from urgent social and economic questions. It worked!

The nation soon had the chance to answer him. In 1880 the Conservatives were swept out of office in a landslide defeat, Gladstone returned for his second premiership and Disraeli, with a year to live, retired to his Hughenden estate.

Trouble abroad

Gladstone meant to retire just two years into his second term, the 50th anniversary of his entering Parliament, but he just couldn't let go.

That five-year spell was unremarkable on the domestic front, although a new Reform Act extended the franchise to agricultural workers (still only the men, of course) and added six million to the number eligible to vote in parliamentary elections.

But it was troublesome in foreign affairs, a low point being the murder of General Gordon, who was defending Khartoum against the Mahdi. Gladstone was blamed for being too slow in sending relief. The Queen sent him a telegram of rebuke which was leaked to the press, and critics turned GOM into MOG – or Murderer of Gordon. *He resigned.*

The Irish question

Cynics who claim that remorselessly pursued principles lose votes and split parties have Peel and the Corn Laws as their Exhibit A, with Gladstone and Irish Home Rule prominently displayed alongside it as Exhibit B.

Gladstone's two brief last terms in office were devoted to a cause he knew was right but for which he had too little support.

The unrest in Ireland had simmered, and sometimes exploded, ever since the seventeenth century, when a Protestant 'ascendancy class' had enforced harsh laws to suppress the Catholic majority.

When, without warning, Gladstone introduced a Home Rule bill in 1886 (a new parliament would be set up in Dublin) the Liberal Unionists under Joseph Chamberlain defected to the Conservatives.

The bill failed in the Commons, after which Gladstone called a general election to settle the matter – and lost.

Lord Randolph Churchill commented bitterly that the Liberals had been 'shivered into fragments to gratify the ambitions of an old man in a hurry'.

Gladstone was six years older still when he came back into power for the last time as head of a minority Liberal government – and he still couldn't let the matter rest.

Through sheer force of will, it seemed, he this time managed to get a new Home Rule bill passed in the Commons, only to see it thrown out in the House of Lords by a crushing majority of 419 to 41. The battle was lost.

He lived on for four years after his resignation in 1894. The eulogies on his death included 'The Burial of Mr Gladstone, the Great Political Hero' by that notoriously dreadful poet of public events, William McGonagall:

Alas! the people now do sigh and moan
For the loss of Wm. Ewart Gladstone,
Who was a very great politician and a moral man,
And to gainsay it there's few people can.

Where they lived

To inspire a pilgrimage with a difference, here are eight former homes of prime ministers open to the public.

CHATSWORTH, Derbyshire
William Cavendish, the fourth Duke of Devonshire and fifth British prime minister, was brought up and educated in one of the country's great stately piles. It was he who employed the landscape gardener Capability Brown to create the park and gardens we see today. He also had parts of a local village demolished to improve the view.

WENTWORTH WOODHOUSE, Yorkshire
The Marquess of Rockingham's father rebuilt the original Jacobean house here, and the prime minister developed it into the largest private residence in the UK: the east front, at 185m (606ft) is said to be the longest country façade in Europe. After the Second World War the Labour government oversaw open cast mining right up to the house. In 2016 a tribunal ruled that structural damage to the house wasn't caused by the mining, but the Conservative government announced a £7.6 million investment towards restoring the house and grounds.

EUSTON HALL, Suffolk
John Evelyn and William Kent had both reshaped the gardens here before the third Duke of Grafton (our eleventh premier) brought in Capability Brown, who introduced a large lake and a weir. The house has a fine art collection.

APSLEY HOUSE, London
Built by Robert Adam in the 1770s, and otherwise known as Number One, London,* the Duke of Wellington's base in the capital stands in proud isolation at Hyde Park Corner. Owned by English Heritage, and officially named the Wellington Museum, it displays the Iron Duke's art collection and other memorabilia.

HOWICK HALL, Northumberland
Earl Grey, who introduced the Great Reform Bill, enlarged the Georgian house, but as that's closed to the public it's in the gardens and arboretum that you'll have to imagine him keeping you company. There are displays telling his story – including the fact that the family missed out on a fortune by failing to register the trade mark for the famous tea.

---

* To the local postmen, though, it's 149 Piccadilly.

HUGHENDEN MANOR, Buckinghamshire

Disraeli had to borrow money from friends in order to buy his Georgian home in the country and transform it into a Gothic creation (complete with battlements) which the architectural historian Nikolaus Pevsner described as 'excruciating'. Dizzy himself thought it wonderfully romantic, and with a poor sense of history claimed that it had been restored to what it was 'before the civil war'. When the National Trust acquired the house in 1947 it discovered that during the Second World War it has been a secret intelligence base with the code-name Hillside.

HATFIELD HOUSE, Hertfordshire

Robert Cecil, the first Earl of Salisbury and chief minister to James I, built this 'prodigy house' – that's to say a great, showy palace of a place – in 1611. The third Marquess of Salisbury, who served as prime minister three times, was a shy man who liked to spend as much time as possible in his ancestral home. Its original Jacobean features include the elaborately carved wooden grand staircase and a rare stained glass window in the private chapel. The seventeenth century gardens were laid out by John Tradescant the Elder and extend over 42 acres (170,000 sq m).

CHARTWELL, Kent

Winston Churchill tops every poll of best prime ministers, and you can explore all aspects of his colourful career at the house he had 'society' architect Philip Tilden transform from a damp and decaying farmhouse (some of it dating from

the time of Henry VIII) into the comfortable home in which 'Winnie' and his wife Clemmie would live for forty years.

The place is much as they knew it, because she left most of the contents as well as personal memorabilia to the National Trust.* There's a large display of Churchill's letters, books, medallions and uniforms in the house, and a collection of his paintings (he was a keen and considerable artist) in the studio outside.

The man himself would also have you admire some of the brick walls he built in the garden: he was, proudly, a card-carrying member of the Amalgamated Union of Bricklayers.

* In 1975 it was designated a World Heritage Site.

6 A fully equipped
duke costs just as
much to keep up as
two dreadnoughts. 9

CHAPTER SIX

A GOAT-FOOTED BARD

In sharp contrast to the sternly moralistic Gladstone, the most charismatic premier in the early decades of the twentieth century was a man who many distrusted but nobody could possibly ignore.

David Lloyd George (1863–1945) was a Welsh firebrand, a lawyer turned Liberal politician nurtured by a rich nonconformist culture to conduct an outsider's assault on what he saw as the forces of reaction – including the House of Lords. His achievements included helping create the forerunner of the modern welfare state and leading the country to victory in the First World War.

A narrow escape

The Boer War of 1899–1902, prosecuted by Lord Salisbury* and his colonial secretary Joseph Chamberlain, was at first popular with the public, giving the Conservatives victory in the 'Khaki Election' of 1900.

The Liberal leader Sir Henry Campbell-Bannerman (or CB, as he liked to be known) was condemned as 'a cad, a coward and a murderer' for opposing it, while Lloyd George took his life in his hands when he gave a rousing anti-war speech in Birmingham (Chamberlain's home turf) and – with the crowd yelling 'Traitor!' and 'Kill him!' – had to escape disguised as a police officer.

British cruelty towards the enemy, creating concentration camps in which large numbers of men, women and children died of disease, turned public sentiment towards the Liberal view, and CB achieved reconciliation with the Boers when he became prime minister.

* His Christian name was Robert, and the saying 'Bob's your uncle' is said to derive from the appointment of his nephew, the inexperienced Arthur Balfour, as chief secretary for Ireland.

Some called him the Welsh Wizard, and he certainly tended to cast a spell over people. Here's the economist John Maynard Keynes:

> How can I convey to the reader who does not know him any impression of this extraordinary figure of our time, this siren, this goat-footed bard, this half-human visitor to our age from the hag-ridden magic and enchanted woods of Celtic antiquity?

However much his low church background inspired his radicalism, however, it imposed few inconvenient restraints on his personal behaviour.

- He was a notorious womaniser,* who almost failed in his first attempt to become a Liberal candidate when it came out that he had 'fathered a child on a very charming widow in Caernarvon', and whose secretary, Frances Stevenson, was his mistress for thirty years

* His principal private secretary, A.J. Sylvester, wasn't surprised about his appeal to women after once seeing him in the buff: 'There he stood as naked as when he was born with the biggest organ I have ever seen. It resembled a donkey's more than anything.'

- He was one of three Liberal ministers who in 1912 bought shares in Marconi, knowing that the company was about to be awarded a lucrative government contract. He was cleared on a technicality, but the public was outraged

- As prime minister he used the seedy John Maundy Gregory (who was later jailed) to sell knighthoods and other honours for cash that ended up in the Liberal Party coffers and his own pockets

Stanley Baldwin's verdict was that he had 'a morally disintegrating effect' on everyone who dealt with him.

The People's Budget

Lloyd George's reforming zeal was given full rein when he served as Asquith's chancellor of the exchequer between 1906 and 1914.

The crunch came in 1909 when he delivered what became known as the People's Budget – knowing that he faced an almighty battle with the House of Lords.

'Five hundred men chosen at random from the ranks of the unemployed.'

Lloyd George on the House of Lords

To raise money for a wide range of measures designed to improve the lot of the poor, sick and needy, he proposed new taxes on the land and income of the rich.

'This is a war budget,' he declared. 'It is for raising money to wage implacable warfare against poverty and squalidness.'

The Lords duly vetoed the budget, and Asquith called two general elections in quick succession in an attempt to establish public support for his welfare reforms.

Lloyd George, meanwhile, enjoyed deriding the upper chamber in his speeches.

'A fully equipped duke costs just as much to keep up as two dreadnoughts,' he quipped – his budget was also designed to boost the country's military capability – and he was 'much less easy to scrap'.

The Liberal reforms perhaps seem timorous by later standards, but they were revolutionary then – and all the more surprising for not having appeared in the party manifesto. Here are just a few of them:

- Old age pensions were introduced for those over 70, although they had to be 'of good character' and to have worked 'to their full potential'

- Health insurance and a tax allowance for children helped families on low incomes

- Free school meals were introduced, although the scheme didn't become compulsory until 1914

- Labour exchanges were set up, and were soon putting thousands into work each day

- A Probation Act introduced a new service to provide supervision in the community for young offenders rather than prison

A drastic solution to the impasse had been proposed by Earl Grey many years before: to create hundreds of new reform-friendly peers.

When George V, now on the throne, agreed to implement this idea the Lords backed down, and Lloyd George got his budget through.

But the Liberals, emboldened by this success, now went much further. Their Parliament Act of 1911 deprived the Lords of their absolute sanction over legislation passed in the Commons, and it thereby changed the balance of power between the two chambers for ever.

War and peace

When the First World War broke out Lloyd George was still chancellor, but he would take over the top job when it became clear that the prime minister wasn't up to it.

Asquith was a strange character, intellectually outstanding but emotionally needy. His second wife had to put up with his attachment to a constant stream of young female attendants (his harem, she called them), and in 1912 he became almost maniacally obsessed with the 25-year-old socialite Venetia Stanley, writing her around 600 letters over three years – some of them while presiding over meetings of his Cabinet.

He was distraught when Venetia announced, out of the blue, that she was marrying the soon to be secretary of state for India, Edwin Montagu.

In 1916 the war was going badly. With Asquith falling into the bottle (his son had been killed in action at the Somme), his colleagues called time on his leadership.

The Coupon Election

Lloyd George was the obvious replacement and, at the head of a coalition with Bonar Law's Conservatives, he saw the war to a successful conclusion.

At his moment of triumph, however, he effectively destroyed his party.

He called a general election for 1918, sending letters of endorsement (known as 'coupons') to candidates who supported a continued power-sharing with the Conservatives. Many Liberal MPs refused to back him – and, with the coalition winning the Coupon Election by a landslide, most of them lost their seats.

It brought about the greatest party split since Peel's Corn Laws and Gladstone's Home Rule – and the Liberals would never again be a major political force.

The Balfour Declaration

The support of Lloyd George's government for 'Jewish Zionist aspirations' was expressed by the Foreign Secretary, Arthur Balfour, in a famous 'declaration' of 1917:

'His Majesty's Government view with favour the establishment in Palestine of a national home for the Jewish people and will use their best endeavours to facilitate the achievement of this object, it being clearly understood that nothing shall be done which may prejudice the civil and religious rights of existing non-Jewish communities in Palestine, or the rights and political status enjoyed by Jews in any other country.'

The short-term aim of the declaration was to win Jewish support for the war effort, particularly in America, but the vagueness of its wording has been blamed for the much longer-term Israeli-Palestinian conflict.

The Irish Question

Lloyd George adopted a stick-and-carrot approach to the troubles in Ireland.

After the Easter Rising of 1916 – the bloody insurrection in Dublin by republican freedom fighters – the government executed the ringleaders, and Lloyd George further inflamed passions by attempting to extend conscription to Ireland shortly before the end of the war.

In 1920 he fondly thought his Government of Ireland Act (or Fourth Home Rule Bill), had seen off the IRA threat by partitioning the country into North and South.

As violence intensified in the South, Lloyd George's secretary of state for war, Winston Churchill, established the Royal Irish Constabulary Special Reserve, a force of temporary constables better known as the Black and Tans because of the colour of their uniform.

They became hated for their brutality – and Lloyd George left office in 1922 with the Irish Question still far from finding its answer.

Aftermath

The beneficiary of the Liberals' collapse was the Labour Party, but it was a wretched time in which to rise to power.

First, a salute to the first ever Labour prime minister. James Ramsay MacDonald, (1866–1937), born in a two-bedroom cottage in Lossiemouth, Scotland, was the illegitimate son of a servant, Annie Ramsay, and a labourer on the same farm, John MacDonald, who soon disappeared without trace.

As a young man he moved to London, where he joined various socialist organisations and became a freelance journalist. His first shot at entering parliament, in 1895, ended in failure as far as the voting went (he came bottom of the poll) but success in that he was given a campaign donation by a wealthy young woman he would later go on to marry.

MacDonald was a sharp operator, negotiating a secret pact with the Liberals not to compete for votes in critical seats, and in 1906 Labour's tally of MPs leapt from just two to 29.

One of these was MacDonald himself, but he had to suffer some sharp reversals before he emerged as the leader of his party.

The first of these was the death of his wife, leaving him devastated and with the care of five young children. The second was his principled opposition to the First World War, which lost him his seat in the 1918 general election.*

Room at the top

When he returned to parliament in 1922 the Labour Party had as many as 142 MPs and he was again its leader. Two years later Baldwin called an election and MacDonald emerged as the head of a minority Labour government.

That heady success lasted for less than a year, but in 1929, though still without a majority, Labour became for the very first time the party with the largest number of seats. Back into Downing Street came the willing MacDonald.

* It also cost him his membership of the Moray Golf Club at Lossiemouth, its members alleging that his anti-war stance damaged the club's character.

Events of dreadful proportions now conspired to test his mettle:

- **Within months of his returning to office the Wall Street Crash triggered the start of the Great Depression**

- **By the end of 1930 unemployment had risen from a million to two and a half million, or one in five of the workforce**

- **Macdonald's chancellor, Philip Snowden, decided on an austerity package which included cutting unemployment benefits**

A run on the pound in August 1931 brought matters to a head. As the cabinet couldn't agree among themselves on further slashes to benefits in order to bolster international confidence in the economy, MacDonald and his ministers offered their resignations to the King.

George's reaction was to ask MacDonald to stay on to lead a national government – and the Labour leader, though ill and exhausted, decided that this was the patriotic thing to do.

It wrecked his party!

Absent friends

A prime minister needs friends when the going gets tough, and MacDonald had never cultivated the left wing of his party.

Indeed, members of his cabinet and their wives, far from being revolutionary, seemed excessively gratified by their rise to the top and were desperate to be seen at their respectable best on public occasions.

Policy-wise he had always been cautious: he had kept Labour out of the Communist International; he had opposed the National Strike in 1926; and he had responded to the Great Depression with savage budget cuts that hit the working classes rather than opting for Keynesian expansion.

His image in the party wasn't helped by his known penchant for grand Conservative ladies. He had a fawning platonic relationship with the society hostess Lady Londonderry (he referred to himself as her 'attendant ghillie'), and wrote a stack of letters to the beautiful Lady Margaret Sackville, daughter of an earl, who three times turned down his proposals of marriage.

Yes, we have another of those ruinous splits to report. Anything the Liberals and the Conservatives could do, Labour was quite capable of matching. In the 1931 election the party was completely trounced, and it knew who to blame.

In fact so furious were MacDonald's MPs that they expelled him and Snowden from the party.

He soldiered on in the post until standing down on health grounds in 1935, a capable, well-meaning but ultimately pathetic character vilified by his own party as a traitor, as he still is by many today.

Labour would have to wait another ten years to regain power – and then they *would* know how to use it...

<blockquote>
I have nothing to offer but blood, toil, tears and sweat.
</blockquote>

CHAPTER SEVEN

THE BULLDOG
AND
THE MOUSE

O f all the politicians who have followed one another into the highest office of the land, none have been as sharply varied in both their characters and the nature of their considerable achievements as Winston Churchill and Clement Attlee.

While the ebullient, adventurous, cigar-toting British bulldog needs no introduction, few have an image of the self-effacing man sneeringly dismissed by a rival as 'a little mouse'. Yet while one pugnaciously led his nation to victory in war, the other just as decisively reshaped it during the ensuing years of peace.

Backstories

Churchill (1874–1965) and Attlee (1883–1967) came from completely different backgrounds and entered politics in completely different ways.

ORIGINS
- A descendant of the Duke of Marlborough, and the son of the Conservative minister Lord Randolph, Churchill was born at Blenheim Palace.

- Attlee was born in Putney to a middle-class family, his father Henry a solicitor.

EDUCATION
- After an unhappy time at Harrow, Churchill entered the Royal Military Academy at Sandhurst.

- Attlee went to Haileybury College and then to University College Oxford, reading history.

SPORT
- Churchill played polo and was a champion fencer.

- Attlee enjoyed billiards and cricket, and played football for non-league club Fleet Town.

EARLY CAREERS

- Churchill was a soldier and a journalist, and he sometimes combined the two while putting himself recklessly in harm's way. He made a dramatic escape from prison during the Boer War, returning home a hero, and wrote up his derring-do experiences in a series of books.

- Attlee trained as a barrister but had no interest in a legal career. He volunteered at a club for working-class boys in the East End of London, and in the summer of 1911 toured Essex and Somerset on a bicycle explaining Lloyd George's National Insurance Act at public meetings. The following year he became a lecturer at the London School of Economics.

INTO POLITICS

- Churchill saw himself as a great leader from the start, and by 1900 he was an MP, winning an Oldham seat in the Khaki Election.

- Attlee originally thought of himself as a moderate Conservative, but his first-hand experience of abject poverty in the East End made him, as he later wrote, 'an enthusiastic convert to Socialism'. He became mayor of Stepney in 1919 and MP for the borough three years later.

Rollercoaster

Churchill's route to the premiership is best described as chaotic.

- He twice switched parties, from the Conservatives to the Liberals and back again ('ratted and re-ratted' as he put it himself)

- As First Lord of the Admiralty during the First World War he was accounted responsible for the disastrous Gallipoli Campaign, and Asquith fired him

- He angered suffragettes over his lukewarm support for votes for women, and one of them horse-whipped him

- He made enemies of striking miners and dockers, his deployment of troops on the streets while Chancellor during the General Strike provoking his premier, Stanley Baldwin, to growl 'He thinks he is Napoleon'

But a Napoleon was exactly what Britain needed during the dark days of the Second World War.

In 1939 Churchill was in the semi-retirement of what he called his 'wilderness years'. Turned out of government when Labour took power ten years earlier, he had remained an MP but retreated to Chartwell to paint, build walls, write books and (of course, always in readiness for the call) to entertain influential friends and agitate in letters to the press for the country to prepare itself for a war he thought inevitable.

Opposing his own party's softly-softly approach to the Hitler threat almost brought about his de-selection by Tories in his Epping seat in 1938, and he survived by a vote of around two-to-one.

But he was simply too experienced to leave on the sidelines when the crunch came, and Chamberlain brought him into the cabinet in his old post as First Lord of the Admiralty.

'And so it was,' he wrote, 'that I came again to the room I had quitted in pain and sorrow almost exactly a quarter of a century before.'

The news was flashed around the Fleet by telegram: 'Winston is back.'

When Chamberlain stood down as prime minister in May 1940, chastened by a failed attempt to dislodge the Germans from Norway, many Conservatives and George VI would rather have had the foreign secretary, Lord Halifax, take over than an infuriating, unpredictable maverick who had long been sniping at the government from the sidelines.

Halifax, though, decided that a coalition government couldn't be run from the Lords, and so it was that Churchill, at the age of 64, at last assumed the mantle he felt he had always been destined to wear.

Inspiration

His tactics were sometimes questioned, but what he offered above all was an eloquent defiance which sustained the morale of the people at a time when defeat to an enemy he pronounced as the 'Natsies' seemed more likely than not.

'I have nothing to offer,' he told the Commons on his first appearance as prime minister, 'but blood, toil, tears and sweat.'

Words of defiance

'You ask, what is our policy? I will say: it is to wage war, by sea, land and air, with all our might and with all the strength that God can give us: to wage war against a monstrous tyranny, never surpassed in the dark, lamentable catalogue of human crime.

'You ask, what is our aim? I can answer in one word: it is victory, victory at all costs, victory in spite of all terror, victory, however long and hard the road may be.'

'We shall fight on the beaches, we shall fight on the landing grounds, we shall fight in the fields and in the streets, we shall fight in the hills. We shall never surrender.'

'Hitler knows that he will have to break us in this island or lose the war. If we can stand up to him, all Europe may be free, and the life of the world will move forward into broad, sunlit uplands.'

'Let us therefore brace ourselves to our duty and so bear ourselves that if the British Commonwealth and Empire lasts for a thousand years, men will still say, "This was their finest hour".'

The war took its toll on him, physically and mentally (throughout his life he was dogged by depression), and he was by turns brilliantly charismatic and, fuelled by champagne, brandy and cigars, shamblingly forgetful.

In 1942 he even had to suffer a two-day censure debate in parliament when a group of cross-party MPs put forward a motion of 'no confidence in the central direction of the war'.

A new world

Eventual victory would become Churchill's 'finest hour' as well as the nation's and, for all his failings, he's regarded as among the foremost in our pantheon of prime ministers.

He was ill-prepared, however, for the peace that followed.

Clement Attlee, the Labour leader since 1935, was deputy prime minister in the wartime coalition, dealing with domestic affairs while the great man dramatised on the world stage. He was much the better prepared for the election called for July 1945.

Churchill, who once patronisingly described Attlee as 'a modest man who has plenty to be modest about', got off on the wrong foot in a pre-election radio broadcast.

He claimed that Socialist policy was 'abhorrent to the British ideas of freedom' and gave the chilling warning that 'they would have to fall back on some sort of Gestapo'.

Attlee's response was devastating:

> When I listened to the prime minister's speech last night, in which he gave such a travesty of the policy of the Labour Party, I realised at once what was his object. He wanted the electors to understand how great is the difference between Winston Churchill, the great leader in war of a united nation, and Mr Churchill, the party leader of the Conservatives.
>
> He feared lest those who had accepted his leadership in war might be tempted out of gratitude to follow him further. I thank him for having disillusioned them so thoroughly. The voice we heard last night was that of Mr Churchill, but the mind was that of [the *Daily Express* proprietor] Lord Beaverbrook.

Labour swept to victory, its 393 MPs opposed by only 213 Conservatives.

Attlee's government would help set up NATO, create an independent India and Pakistan, and withdraw Britain from Palestine at the birth of the state of Israel, while on the home front it introduced the most sweeping set of reforms the country had ever seen.

- The National Health Service, with free health care for all

- A National Insurance Act, giving a wide range of benefits, including retirement pensions, sickness and widows' benefits and unemployment benefit in return for compulsory contributions

- Nationalisation of the coal, rail, electricity and haulage industries

- The Town and Country Planning Act, requiring planning permission for land development

- The creation of National Parks and Areas of Outstanding Natural Beauty

Churchill would have the last laugh, failing in health though he was, when the Conservatives came back into power in 1951, but Attlee's legacy was secure.

He retired four years later and was given various honours, including an earldom. A life-long lover of poetry, he wrote a limerick for his brother Tom in which he allowed himself a little gentle pride.

> Few thought he was even a starter
> There were those who thought themselves
>> smarter
> But he ended PM
> CH and OM
> An earl and a knight of the garter.

In times of trouble

Crises for prime ministers come in a wide variety of guises...

Anthony Eden's wound was self-inflicted. In 1956 the Egyptian dictator, President Nasser, nationalised the Suez Canal. Britain and France secretly backed an invasion by Israel and then, after calling for a ceasefire, sent in their own paratroopers.

Despite an immediate tactical success, the overall strategy failed disastrously. For one thing, Nasser blocked the canal so that no ships could use it. More significantly, the action was condemned by the US, the Soviet Union and the United Nations, and their joint political pressure forced the invaders to withdraw.

This debacle is widely regarded as marking the end of Britain as a world power. Eden compounded his disgrace by lying to the House of Commons about his intrigue with Israel. In January the following year, plagued by ill health, he both resigned as premier and gave up his parliamentary seat.

*

Harold Macmillan was a humorous fellow, who once quipped (referring to his reading habits) that he liked nothing better than going to bed with a Trollope.* Unfortunately it was a scandal involving a pair of good-time girls that hastened his downfall.

The so-called Profumo Affair that surfaced in 1963 provided the public with wonderfully rich entertainment. It emerged that the Minister for War, John Profumo, had enjoyed sex parties organised by the society osteopath Stephen Ward at Cliveden, Lord Astor's country estate in Buckinghamshire.

Profumo's occasional mistress, the leggy former topless showgirl and would-be model Christine Keeler, had shared her favours with the Soviet naval attaché (and intelligence officer) Yevgeny Ivanov, raising fears that her pillow-talk might have betrayed British secrets to the Cold War enemy.

It was lying to the Commons about sleeping with Keeler that forced Profumo's resignation and disappearance from public life.

---

* *A long-running sadness in his life was the affair of his wife Dorothy with the hedonistic, bisexual Tory backbencher Robert Boothby.*

> 'A week is a long time in politics.'
>
> *Harold Wilson*

The saddest outcome was Ward's suicide, the most amusing the court appearance of Keeler's friend Mandy Rice-Davies ('Randy Mice' to the wags), who responded to Astor's denial of sleeping with her with the famous line 'He would, wouldn't he?'

Macmillan's authority was diminished by the scandal and, a sick man, he stood down soon afterwards.

*

They called **James Callaghan** 'Sunny Jim', but his genial nature rebounded against him when his response to a financial meltdown in 1979 was caricatured in the tabloid press as 'Crisis – What Crisis?'

This was during the so-called Winter of Discontent. The British economy had been languishing throughout the previous Wilson and Heath premierships, but it now took a turn for the worse, and Callaghan imposed savage spending cuts in order to get a loan from the International Monetary Fund.

The trade unions, a forceful power in the political landscape, demanded large pay increases, and public sector workers went on strike when they were refused. Rubbish began to pile up in the streets and hospitals adopted an 'emergency cases only' policy.

The government had suffered a steady trickle of by-election defeats and, with their majority wilting, were reduced to wheeling sick MPs into the Commons chamber. In late March they narrowly lost a vote of no confidence, and Callaghan called a general election.

To the suggestion by his senior official Bernard Donoughue that Labour might sneak in again, he gave a head-shaking reply:

> There are times, perhaps once every thirty years, when there's a sea-change in politics. It then doesn't matter what you say or what you do. There is a shift in what the public wants and what it approves of. I suspect there is now such a change – and it is for Mrs Thatcher.

How right he was!

' You turn if you want to – the lady's not for turning. '

CHAPTER EIGHT

THATCHER'S CHILDREN

She was Britain's first woman prime minister, she was so distinctive an operator that she gave her name to an 'ism' and she polarised the public between devoted followers and rabid enemies as few had done before.

Her policies and personality were equally divisive. She drove an iconoclastic right-wing assault on the prevailing political consensus with a determination that brooked no dissent. Happy to make enemies of those unwise enough to oppose her, she refused to swerve from any path she had chosen – and at the last paid the price for her rigidity.

The Gang of four

Here's another party split for your growing collection. Thatcher's premiership provoked a swing to the left in the Labour Party under the leadership of Michael Foot. It was a swing too far for some of its stalwarts, and in 1981 a quartet of former cabinet ministers broke away to form the Social Democratic Party (SDP).

In their Limehouse Declaration the so-called Gang of Four (Roy Jenkins, David Owen, Shirley Williams and Bill Rogers) declared that 'a handful of trade union leaders can now dictate the choice of a future prime minister', and they called for 'a new start in British politics'.

The SDP won some notable early by-election victories, but its greatest success was pushing Labour further to the right, leading to the eventual election of Tony Blair as prime minister.

The original SDP merged with the Liberals in 1988 to form the Liberal Democrats, although (split and split again) Owen and some other MPs formed a breakaway party and kept the name.

Margaret Thatcher (1925–2013) looked back with disdain on two previous periods of Labour government: Attlee's with its nationalisations and Wilson's with its passing of liberal laws on homosexuality, abortion, capital punishment and theatre censorship in the 'permissive society' of the Sixties.

Here's what she told *Woman's Own* magazine:

> I think we have gone through a period when too many children and people have been given to understand 'I have a problem, it is the government's job to cope with it!' 'I am homeless, the government must house me!' And so they're casting their problems on society, and who is society? There is no such thing! There are individual men and women and there are families, and no government can do anything except through people, and people look to themselves first.

Thatcherism, in short, proclaimed the mantra 'private, good; public bad'. She privatised a wide range of industries and, in order to create a 'property owning democracy', had council houses sold to tenants at a cheap rate while not allowing local authorities to replace them.

Regarding trade unions as 'the enemy within' and 'dangerous to liberty', she crippled their ability to hold strikes and to engage in political action.

Not for turning

Early in her premiership, with unemployment rising to three million, she made a defiant speech at the Conservative Party Conference: 'You turn if you want to – the lady's not for turning.'

Written for her by the playwright Ronald Millar, it contained both a pun on 'U-turn' and a reference to Christopher Fry's play *The Lady's not for Burning* – something that needed to be explained to her.

This was par for the course. She was notably lacking both in a sense of humour and cultural references. After Callaghan had compared himself to Moses, her speech-writer gave her the quip 'Keep taking the tablets' (*Exodus* 34:1, should you need to check it yourself), but she had to be coached against replacing 'tablets' with 'pills'.

She was also blind to double entendres. She relied heavily on William Whitelaw, the Conservative's deputy leader throughout her almost twelve years in office, and once exclaimed warmly – and certainly without the invisible wink that almost anyone else would have intended – 'Everyone needs a Willie!'

Whitelaw was an exception in earning her esteem. There are many stories of her kindness towards people lower in the social scale, but to her cabinet she could be harshly overbearing.

Among the vegetables

ITV's satirical programme *Spitting Image*, with its brilliant and innovative use of puppetry by Peter Fluck and Roger Law, enjoyed playing up the dominance of Margaret Thatcher over the compliant male colleagues in her cabinet.

In one scene she sits with them in a restaurant and orders a steak.

'What about the vegetables?' the waitress asks.

'Oh,' she says, 'they'll have the same as me.'

These were the so-called Wets, who disliked her more extreme free-market policies but timorously failed to oppose them to her face.*

falklands ahoy!

At a low point in her ratings nationally, she turned her fortunes with a war. In 1982 the British overseas territory of the Falkland Islands – an archipelago some 8,000 miles away off the coast of South America, and home to a scattered population of a few thousand sheep farmers – was invaded by Argentina.

Many thought it quixotic to send an armed force all that way to liberate a place of so little significance, but that's what Thatcher did – and a swift victory revived her flagging reputation.

She was the Iron Lady (a term first used about her by the Soviet Union) and to those who metaphorically fell at her feet she had become a Britannia figure.

* *Edward Heath never forgave her for ousting him as leader of the party. After she resigned he denied saying 'Rejoice! Rejoice!' when what he had really said was 'Rejoice! Rejoice! Rejoice!'*

She wasn't a beauty, but she turned some grown men to jelly.

- Her former minister John Selwyn Gummer: 'She had beautiful hands and lovely ankles, and she knew how to use them.'

- President Mitterand of France: 'She has the eyes of Caligula and the mouth of Marilyn Monroe.'

Orgreave

Fresh from surviving the Brighton bombing, with her never-say-die image given a fresh shine, she took on the nation's coal miners who were striking over the closure of their pits.

When, in June 1984, mounted police and officers with dogs violently attacked miners at Orgreave colliery in South Yorkshire, it wasn't only the usual suspects who protested.

The 90-year-old Harold Macmillan (now Lord Stockton), said 'It breaks my heart to see – and I cannot interfere – what is happening in our country today.'

It was, Macmillan said (in his maiden speech in the House of Lords), a terrible strike 'by the best men in the world, who beat the Kaiser's and Hitler's armies and never gave in. It is pointless and we cannot afford that kind of thing.'

But the miners were routed: the indomitable 'Leaderine' had won again.

The poll tax

Thatcher strutted the world stage with US President Ronald Reagan, denouncing the Soviet bloc before it disintegrated, but came to grief over a domestic crisis of her own making.

In 1989 she proposed that the system of paying for local services through rates based on house values should be replaced by the community charge, a flat rate per head which meant the poor would pay exactly the same as the rich, and in many cases would be much worse off than before. It was known as the poll tax.

There were riots in towns and cities up and down the land.

Thatcher was too wedded to her poll tax to allow compromise. The Wets were, at last, emboldened to act, and she was pushed aside for John Major – who promptly ditched it in favour of a new council tax.

New Labour

In 1997 the 43-year-old Tony Blair arrived in Downing Street with a thumping 179-seat majority over the Conservatives.

He could, during his first days in power, have launched a full-throttle socialist programme with no danger of defeat, but the Iron Lady had changed everything. Blair was so in awe of her legacy that he had rebranded his party as New Labour – a signal that there would be no return to the days of strong unions, nationalisation and taxes which hurt the rich.

Blair and his press secretary Alastair Campbell would spend large amounts of energy during his three terms in office courting positive coverage in the right-wing *Daily Mail*. The message was clear: the politicians were all Thatcher's children now.

Peace in Ireland

Nobody dared claim, after centuries of strife, that the Good Friday Agreement had solved the problem once and for all, but it was undoubtedly a major step in the long and tortuous Northern Ireland peace process.

Tony Blair signed it on behalf of the British government in April 1998, and the following month it was approved by voters across the island of Ireland in two referendums – with the Democratic Unionist Party (DUP) the only major political group in Northern Ireland to oppose it.

The Agreement created new institutions between Northern Ireland and the Republic of Ireland, and between the Republic and the UK, with a devolved form of government based in the Northern Ireland Assembly at Stormont.

Blair was known for his effective, if glib, one-liners, and before signing the document with the Irish taoiseach Bertie Ahern, he appeared to parody himself: 'A day like today is not a day for soundbites,' he declared, 'but I feel the hand of history upon our shoulder.'

This isn't to deny that the Blair government chalked up some genuine achievements from a left-wing perspective.

- **The introduction of the minimum wage**

- **More money for the NHS, with cuts in waiting times; and for schools, with cuts in class sizes**

- **The Sure Start Scheme to improve the lot of children through childcare, early education and health and family support**

- **The Human Rights Act and Freedom of Information Act**

- **Devolved government for Scotland and Wales as well as for Northern Ireland**

His cabinet included more women than ever before and the first openly gay minister. New legislation improved the lot of lesbian, gay and transgender people – discrimination in the workplace was outlawed – while the Civil Partnership Act gave gay couples the same rights as married heterosexual couples.

Bush's buddy

This would all be forgotten in the years to come thanks to his sending British troops into Iraq in support of the gung-ho US President George W. Bush.

The devastating '9-11' attack by al-Qaeda on the New York Twin Towers in 2001 provoked Bush to a chaotic 'war on terror', and the Prime Minister was a willing accomplice.

An abiding image is of Tony Blair swaggering from his shoulders alongside the Texan President at a Camp David meeting, fingers tucked into pockets as if ready to pull a pair of pistols from their holsters.

Iraq's Saddam Hussein, although a vicious and evil leader, had no connection with al-Qaeda, and UN weapons inspectors determined that he had, as he claimed, already obediently destroyed his 'weapons of mass destruction'.

Blair and his team nevertheless persuaded themselves that what became known as the 'dodgy dossier' of flimsy evidence concocted against Hussein justified an invasion.

The Iraq War, though successful in military terms, was otherwise a disaster. No thought had been given to how the country should be restructured in its aftermath, and by shaking up the delicate balances of power in the region it ensured further bloodshed for decades to come.

After Blair stepped down from the premiership he further tarnished his image by earning vast sums on lecture tours around the globe, often schmoozing with leaders whose tarnished reputations ill-matched the high-minded persona he liked to present to the world.

This meant that when he sought to influence public opinion at home, as in the tangled debate about Brexit, his was a voice crying in the wilderness...

' Once and for all
we are really in
Europe and ready
to go ahead. '

CHAPTER NINE

TROUBLE WITH EUROPE

W e may form a part of it geographically, but to most Britons Europe is a place we go to – a short hop across the Channel, true, but unquestionably 'over there'.

For many of our early prime ministers it was the scene of fragile alliances and, very often, of bloody conflict. After the Second World War its nation states came together through what is now the European Union to achieve a long period of peace and economic stability, but although Britain eventually became a member of the club, it never felt quite at home.

What they said

Winston Churchill 1946: 'We must build a kind of United States of Europe' in order to 'recreate the European family'.

Harold Macmillan 1961: 'I believe that our right place is in the vanguard of the movement towards the greater unity of the free world, and that we can lead better from within than outside.'

Margaret Thatcher 1988: 'We have not successfully rolled back the frontiers of the state in Britain, only to see them re-imposed at a European level with a European super-state exercising a new dominance from Brussels.'

John Major 1991: 'It is because we care for lasting principles that I want to place Britain at the heart of Europe.'

Tony Blair 2005: 'This is a union of values, of solidarity between nations and people, of not just a common market in which we trade but a common political space in which we live as citizens.'

At first, in 1957, it was the European Economic Community (EEC), with six founder members: Belgium, France, Italy, Luxembourg, the Netherlands and West Germany. Its aim was straightforward: to integrate the economies of Europe.

'Non!'

After an initial lack of interest, Britain twice applied to join – in 1963 (under Macmillan) and 1967 (Wilson) – but on both occasions the French president, Charles de Gaulle, vetoed the move despite the willingness of the other members to support it.

Some aspects of its economy, from its working practices to its agriculture, made Britain and the EEC incompatible, he said, observing (astutely we may say, bearing in mind later developments) that Britain harboured a 'deep-seated hostility' to pan-European projects.

When de Gaulle left office in 1969 the way was at last clear for British entry – and for her prime ministers to drink in turn from the poisoned chalice.

The will of the people

Edward Heath, who as lord privy seal had been Macmillan's negotiator during the UK's first failed attempt to join the EEC, triumphantly took the country into the trading bloc in 1973 – and very soon found out how divisive a move that was.

A man of many parts

A prickly character, and one of four Prime Ministers never to marry, Ted Heath had a full life outside parliament.

He could have been a professional pianist or organist; conducted leading orchestras around the world; was president of the European Community Youth Orchestra; and wrote the book *Music: A Joy for Life*.

He was also the only British prime minister to win an international sporting trophy while in office. He owned a series of racing yachts named *Morning Cloud*, and in 1969 skippered one of them to victory in the gruelling Hobart Sidney race. Two years later he won the Admirals Cup as captain of the British team.

Within two years – by which time Harold Wilson was in power – the public was being asked to decide whether to stay in or to beat a hasty retreat.

In a referendum campaign similar to the Brexit scenario more than forty years later, the man and woman in the street spoke of 'confusing' statistics, got angry with one another and plumped for Yes and No as much for emotional as for practical reasons.

Wilson, who had come back from Brussels with what he described as a better deal for Britain, recommended staying in, but several left-wingers in his cabinet claimed that the EEC was a capitalist club that would destroy jobs.

The new Tory leader, Margaret Thatcher, was at this stage a Europhile: 'Once and for all,' she said, 'we are really in Europe and ready to go ahead.'

The public agreed: they backed staying in by a solid two-thirds majority, only Shetland and the Western Isles voting against.

A handbagging

Thatcher proved much less friendly towards Europe once she was installed in Downing Street. For one thing she thought Britain was paying far too much into the EEC budget – and she took herself off to Fontainebleu in order to (proverbially) 'handbag' President Mitterand.

'I want my money back!' was her down-to-earth public demand.

The result was a 66 per cent 'rebate' – and ill-feeling across the Channel at what it saw as British belligerence.

She signed up for the Single Market, later regretting it, but grew increasingly disturbed – see her quote on page 170 – by visions of a European super-state.

What drove her to undisguised fury was a speech in September 1988 by the president of the European Commission, Jacques Delors, that looked forward, within a period of ten years, to 'the beginnings of a European government'.

The *Sun* would have fun with his name in the famous headline UP YOURS DELORS, while Thatcher's response in the Commons was a brief but emphatic outburst: 'No! No! No!'

The later Tory strife over Europe can be traced back to this moment. Her deputy, Geoffrey Howe, promptly resigned and her successors had to deal with the consequences.

500 million

Britain, Ireland and Denmark joined the EEC in its first wave of expansion in 1973. By the time the Maastricht Treaty created the European Union (EU) in 1992, membership had risen to a dozen, with Greece, Portugal and Spain also now on board.

Eastern Germany (after unification), Austria, Finland and Sweden were the next to join, while the biggest enlargement came in and after 2004, when former Soviet bloc countries signed up.

By 2019 there were 28 member countries of the EU, with a total population of more than 500 million.

The Bastards

Forgive our language, but this is how John Major (caught on camera in an unguarded moment) described those MPs – some of them members of his cabinet – who threatened to tear the Conservatives apart with their constant agitation against the European project.

'Where do you think most of this poison is coming from?' he asked a TV reporter. 'From the dispossessed and the never-possessed. You can think of ex-ministers who are going around causing all sorts of trouble.'

The focal point of Major's problem was the Maastricht Treaty of 1992, which created the European Union and brought about closer integration among member states.

The life peer and former editor of *The Times*, William Rees-Mogg, took legal action against the government in an attempt to prevent the UK signing the treaty.

When this move failed, Major scribbled a note to his private secretary: 'A full gloat is merited.'

Labour had its own divisions, but managed to contain a mounting disaffection with the EU. As chancellor, and then as prime minister, Gordon Brown set such strict conditions on the UK joining the common currency (the Euro), that they would never be met.

Crucially, he thwarted deafening calls for a referendum over the Lisbon Treaty, which created a new EU constitution that its critics alleged gave too much power to Brussels.

David Cameron, who entered Downing Street in 2010, led a Tory party in such unbridled mutiny over Europe that he promised a referendum on Britain's membership should he win a second term in office.

Brexit

He did win; he held the referendum; the public voted narrowly (52 to 48 per cent) to leave the EU; and he immediately resigned.

And so it came about that in 2016 a new prime minister, Theresa May, was charged with achieving the British exit – or Brexit.

The Boris file

One of the problems for Remainers during the Brexit campaign was that for years there had been a constant drip-feed of negative stories about the EU in the British media.

These included countless tall tales about EU practices, many of them filed by the *Daily Telegraph* journalist (and later Tory MP) Boris Johnson when he was the newspaper's Brussels correspondent.

Yarns about standardised condom sizes and bans on British pink sausages, together with others headlined 'Snails are fish, says EU' and 'Brussels recruits sniffers to ensure that Euromanure smells the same', were amusing but false. He likened his work to chucking rocks over a wall and smashing a greenhouse next door.

'Everything I wrote from Brussels was having this amazing, explosive effect on the Tory party,' he said later, 'and it really gave me this I suppose rather weird sense of power.'

There was both disbelief and disapproval in Europe when Theresa May appointed him foreign secretary in 2016.

178

What followed was a crisis of epic proportions. The referendum had offered a crude Yes/No alternative, leaving Britain's future relationship with the EU after Brexit entirely up in the air.

May's way of dealing with this uncertainty will doubtless occupy students of politics for generations to come.

- **She immediately persuaded parliament to invoke Article 50 of the EU treaty, setting the UK's withdrawal in motion, and fixed a date of March 29th, 2019, for leaving**

- **She laid down a set of 'red lines' in her dealings with the EU, prioritising controls on immigration***

- **She brought prominent Leavers into her cabinet to show that she was intent on a 'hard' Brexit with few concessions to Remainers seeking to keep a close relationship with our former allies**

---

* *This had long been an obsession. When home secretary in 2013, she sent vans into London boroughs plastered with the message 'In the UK illegally? Go home or face arrest.'*

- **She called a snap election in June 2017
  in order to see off the doubters – and,
  campaigning disastrously, lost her
  majority in Parliament**

*The agreement she reached with the EU was voted
down by the greatest majority ever suffered by a
British prime minister.*

– The 'soft' Brexiters argued that it cut Britain
off from too many of the benefits, trading and
otherwise, the nation had previously enjoyed.

– The 'hard' Brexiters, among them William
Rees-Mogg's son Jacob, claimed that it wasn't
a clean break at all and said they'd much rather
crash out with no deal at all. (Over the months
several of her ministers, including Boris
Johnson, resigned.)

Having a heads-down, do-it-my-way kind of
personality, Theresa May doggedly pursued
her deal without a hint of compromise to those
who offered it. Her admirers regarded her
tenacity as a virtue, but the common view was
that she had been dealt a terrible hand – and
had played it badly.

TROUBLE WITH EUROPE

After two deadlines passed without progress and a third was agreed with the EU for the end of October, 2019, May resigned as party leader, continuing as prime minister only until a Tory grassroots membership of around 160,000 had chosen her successor from an initial list of eleven hopeful candidates.

The colourful but divisive Boris Johnson emerged as the winner, promising an October Brexit even if that meant bypassing Parliament to pursue the no-deal scenario and dismantling an agreed 'backstop' designed to preserve peace on the border between Northern Ireland and the Republic.

With several ministers immediately resigning, the electorate bitterly divided and economists warning of pending economic disaster, a detached observer – and perhaps the despairing ghost of Robert Walpole – could be forgiven for wondering why anyone should want the wretched job at all.

Glossary

Chartism A movement of the 1830s and 1840s agitating for the reform of parliament.

cornetcy The rank of a commissioned officer in a cavalry troop.

dog Latin A crude version of Latin in other languages.

habeas corpus A writ requiring a person under arrest to be brought into court.

IRA (Irish Republican Army) a paramilitary group of the 20th and 21st centuries seeking the independence of Ireland from British rule.

Jacobism A movement to restore the House of Stuart to the thrones of England, Scotland and Ireland.

Lords spiritual Church of England bishops serving in the House of Lords.

Luddites Originally, textile workers in the early 19th century who destroyed machinery that threatened their jobs.

monetarism an economic theory which prioritises the control by governments of the money in circulation.

pocket/rotten borough Before the Great Reform Act, a parliamentary seat held by one man and/ or having a very small electorate.

Radical An advocate of political or social change.

sinecure A salaried job which requires little or no real work.

Prime Ministers timeline

1721 Robert Walpole is appointed First Lord of the Treasury – and is now recognised as the first of our prime ministers.

1728 John Gay's *The Beggar's Opera* satirises corruption in Walpole's government.

1733 Walpole's Excise Crisis.

1737 Licensing Act controls performance of plays.

1739 The War of Jenkins's Ear.

1756 Start of Seven Years' War under Pitt the Elder.

1757 Admiral Byng executed.

1763 Treaty of Paris cedes French territory to Britain; Bute's cider tax provokes riots.

1765 North imposes Stamp Act on American colonies.

1773 The 'Boston Tea Party'

1782 North resigns over loss of American colonies.

1798 Pitt the Younger duels with George Tierney.

1809 Canning/Castlereagh duel.

1812 Spencer Perceval assassinated in the Commons.

1815 Introduction of the Corn Laws.

1819 Peterloo Massacre in Manchester.

1829 Wellington fights duel with Earl of Wilmington; Peel founds Metropolitan Police Force.

1830 Swing Riots throughout the country; Wellington's London house stoned by a mob.

1832 Gray's Great Reform Bill.

1833 Slave Abolition Act passed.

1834 Poor Law Amendment Act; Peel issues his Tamworth Manifesto and avoids assassination; Houses of Parliament burn down.

1846 Peel reforms Corn Laws and splits the Tories.

1867   Second Reform Bill.

1875   Disraeli buys nation a share in the Suez Canal.

1877   Queen Victoria given title Empress of India.

1878   Start of Gladstone's Midlothian Campaign.

1885   General Gordon killed in siege of Khartoum.

1886   Gladstone's Home Rule Bill.

1894   Electricity installed in Downing Street.

1899–1902   Second Boer War.

1909   Lloyd George's People's Budget.

1911   Parliament Act restricts power of Lords over legislation passed in the Commons.

1914–1918   First World War.

1916   Easter Rising in Ireland.

1917   The Balfour Declaration; Chequers is given to the nation as the prime minister's country residence.

1918   The Coupon Election.

1924   Ramsay MacDonald is the head of Labour's first (minority) government.

1937   Central heating installed in Downing Street.

1939–1945   Second World War.

1940   Winston Churchill becomes prime minister of a wartime coalition government.

1945   Labour, under Attlee, win power and introduce social reforms, including the National Health Service.

1956   Suez Canal crisis.

1963   The Profumo Affair rocks Macmillan's government; de Gaulle rejects Britain's request to join the EEC.

1967   Britain again refused EEC entry.

1973   Edward Heath takes Britain into the EEC.

1979   Margaret Thatcher is the country's first woman prime minister.

1981   Gang of Four break from Labour to form the SDP.

1982 Falklands War.
1984 IRA bombs the Grand Hotel in Brighton; violence at Orgreave Colliery during the miners' strike.
1989 Security gates erected at the end of Downing Street; Thatcher introduces the poll tax.
1991 IRA shell Downing Street.
1992 Maastricht Treaty: EEC becomes the EU.
1997 New Labour wins power under Tony Blair.
1998 The Good Friday Agreement is a major step in the Northern Ireland peace process.
2003 Beginning of the Iraq War.
2016 In a referendum, British public votes to leave the EU; Theresa May becomes prime minister.
2017 May loses her majority in general election.
2019 Boris Johnson becomes prime minister.

*

Additional reading

British Prime Ministers, Robert J. Parker (Amberley)
Gimson's Prime Ministers, Andrew Gimson (Square Peg)
10 Downing Street, Anthony Seldon (HarperCollins)

Among David Arscott's other titles in this series:
    American Presidents and *Churchill*
His fiction includes the satirical political novel
    Lady Thatcher's Wink (Pomegranate Press)

Index